# Find the Motherlode of Wealth in Your Business

# Find the
# Motherlode of Wealth
## in Your Business

### And Outperform Your Competition
### Again and Again, Even in Turbulent Times

**Jay Abraham**   **Carlos Dias**

Creative **Leadership**
FOR TURBULENT TIMES
with **Jay Abraham** and **Carlos Dias**

**Find the Motherlode of Wealth in Your Business**

*And Outperform Your Competition Again and Again, Even in Turbulent Times*

Also available as an audio-visual presentation at:
*http://www.executivelearningsystems.com/motherlode/*

ISBN-10: 0989597601
ISBN-13: 978-0-9895976-0-9

For information contact:
*http://www.abraham.com*
*http://www.carlosdias.com*

# Contents

## PART THREE   The Secret Map   41

## PART FOUR  Uniqueness                                73

# Introduction

**Welcome to our program!** I'm Jay Abraham. Carlos Dias and I are here to talk to you about achieving CEO greatness. You know, like becoming one of those CEOs you read about in the business magazines…

*Jay Abraham*

…that guy who transformed his sluggish family business into a thriving profit-generating machine.

…that gal who repositioned her fuddy-duddy old business to capitalize on exciting new markets and opportunities.

…that CEO who knows in his heart that he has put his organization on a path to solid, secure, sustainable growth – a legacy of wealth for his family now and into the future – even in our fast-changing economy.

That's what CEO greatness looks like, right? But unfortunately, if you're like most CEOs today, that's not your reality at all.

**Walker Leads ABC CO to Profit**

**Obrien Opens a New Window at Acme Glass**

**Patel Sees Nothing But Growth for Transporter LTD**

In this book, Carlos and I discuss the reality that so many CEOs today face, why today's reality is different, and what it will take to transform that reality into opportunity and prosperity for your business.

# PART ONE

## The Challenge

## Meet John

Unfortunately, most CEOs today are like our friend John here. Take a look and see if John's situation sounds familiar.

John heads up a nice, medium-sized, profitable business – about $300M or so in sales last year –  passed down to him from his Dad and his Grandfather who founded the business.

John works long and he works hard. But no matter how hard John tries these days, his business can't seem to get any traction.

This creates a lot of stress for John.

**Pre-2007**

Back in the old, pre-2007 days before the recession, growth was easy to accomplish. Back then, the business would reliably throw off enough profits each year to fund a generous dividend – the dividend that supported his family members and other shareholders very comfortably.

**Post-2007**

But those days are gone. Today's profits are much more modest. John's family shareholders are suffering, and like most families, they don't suffer silently!

The atmosphere is getting more acrimonious. People are losing patience. They are questioning whether John is the right man to lead the business these days. Truth be told, John is wondering the same thing himself.

Today's Schedule:

|  | |
|------|---|
| 8:00 | Production line status |
| 8:45 | Supplier feedback |
| 9:30 | Inventory logistics team |
| 10:45 | Bank re: Q3 Financing |
| Lunch | Board Meeting |
| 2:00 | HR Director: Right size staff? |
| 4:00 | Finalize product decisions |

Not that John and his staff haven't been trying.

In fact, he is juggling so many business-improvement initiatives that he is having trouble keeping them straight.

He spends so much time in meetings about all of those initiatives that sometimes he forgets which meeting he's in!

John knows that he is putting in the effort. But he is concerned that all that effort is earning very modest returns, at best.

# What Keeps John Awake at Night?

It's no wonder that John hasn't been sleeping so well lately. At night he lies awake, wrestling with business problems in his head.

Why is financial performance so dismal? Is the problem his product line? Or should he leave the products alone but expand into new markets?

Maybe he should invest in a benchmarking initiative – like they talked about back in business school. Or maybe he should look into this new social-marketing thing – that's what all the hot, new up-and-coming businesses seem to be doing.

Or then again, maybe he should hire one of the professors from the university to advise him. It would be risky, because there would be no guarantees and it would cost a fortune, but if he *happened* to find someone with the up-to-date industry knowledge and global perspective that he needed, somebody who has a *practical* orientation and hasn't been stuck in an ivory tower all his life, then *maybe* it would work out…

There are so many options these days. Everything is changing so quickly. But that just makes it harder for John to know which way to lead the business.

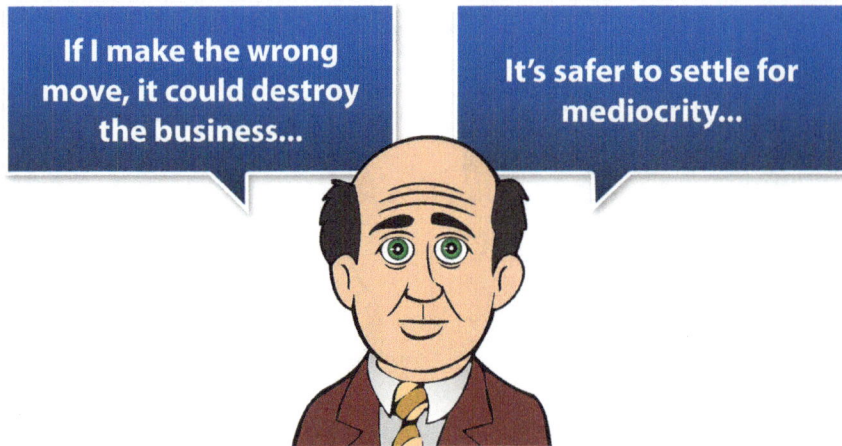

In a confusing world, there is only one thing John is sure of: if he makes the wrong decisions… if he screws up… it will be a disaster for a lot of people – himself, his family, and his employees, too – and it will be all his fault.

So yes, John would like to be a great CEO. But these days, John is settling for mediocrity. He's tired. He's stressed. He's unsure which way to turn… or what to do next.

## The Price of Mediocrity

Frustrated

Disappointed

Confused

Insecure

Overwhelmed

Embarrassed

Exhausted

Stressed

Burdened

Trapped

**Settling for Mediocrity**

Does John's story sound familiar? In today's crazy economy, far too many CEOs find themselves settling for less. But what they fail to realize is that mediocrity comes at a price. And a big one at that!

There are the emotional, psychological, and yes, even physical costs of living with constant disappointment and stress.

There is the embarrassment of letting everyone down – your family, your customers, your employees, other stakeholders, and yourself.

Worst of all is the nightmarish feeling of being trapped in a terrible situation – and not knowing how to escape.

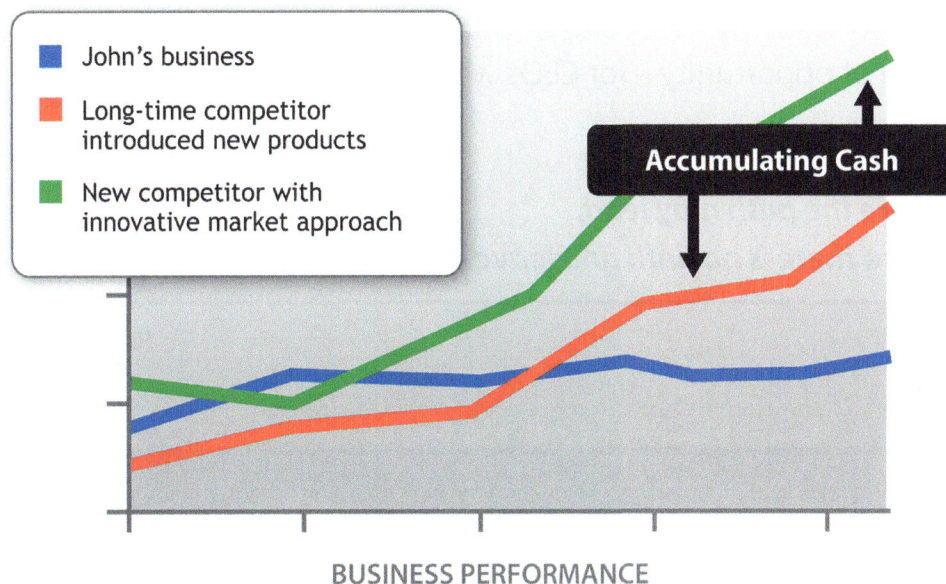

**BUSINESS PERFORMANCE**

There is another price, one that many CEOs fail to recognize.

That's the price you pay in lost opportunity. Because not every business has allowed itself to get stuck. Not every business is wallowing in inertia. In fact, look behind you – because some of the businesses who are succeeding are your competitors. They are finding new ways to engage with customers – your customers. They are finding innovative new products to bring to market – your market. They are accumulating cash – cash that could have been yours – and they soon will be investing it to grow their businesses. **They are gaining on you – and if you continue to stand still, you can be sure they will overtake you!**

# The Quandary

*"When opportunity comes knocking, there is a high cost for not opening the door. You need to be able to recognize opportunity when you see it."*

**JAY ABRAHAM**

So here is the quandary that many CEOs face.

We're living through turbulent times. Turbulent times are scary, because they disrupt the normal, familiar status quo.

But there are two sides to that coin, because an environment that is disrupted is an environment full of opportunity – for CEOs who know where to look.

*"Do not go where the path may lead, go instead where there is no path and leave a trail."*

**RALPH WALDO EMERSON**

Unfortunately, many CEOs – like our friend John, for example – don't recognize the motherlode of hidden wealth that exists in their businesses. They aren't able to see the opportunities for business breakthroughs that are there for the taking, if only they knew where to look – so instead, they keep digging in the same played-out hole that will net them nothing but mediocrity.

## Why Are CEOs Blind to Opportunities?

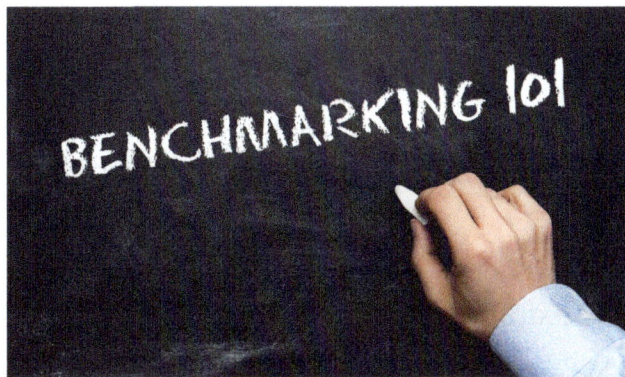

**CEOs have been trained to look backward**

This brings us to the next question. Why? Why are so many CEOs blind to the opportunities all around them?

Sadly, CEOs like John are failing today precisely because they are doing exactly what they were educated and trained to do… and that skill set worked well, as long as they remained in a steady, status quo-driven, non-turbulent environment.

When John went to business school, his professors taught him that business was essentially a zero-sum game. Every market was a pie, with competitors holding fairly fixed slices of that pie. A CEO's job, therefore, was to figure out how to slowly but surely grab an incrementally larger piece of the pie. The way to accomplish that, proven out by case study after case study, was to copy and improve on whatever your competitors were doing. Tinker here. Tinker there. Reorganize and restructure. But base your decisions on hindsight – on whatever was working well for you and your competitors in the past. That made sense back then – because back then, you could safely assume that what was true in your marketplace yesterday would still be true today and tomorrow.

*"In today's dynamic, fast moving non-linear market, benchmarking and traditional management planning models no longer work. Why? These are no more than exercises in extrapolating the status quo and rarely do these pseudo-strategies abandon yesterday, but simply carry it into the future.*

*So why should you benchmark best practices from leading companies when before you master them, they become obsolete?"*

**FINANCIAL TIMES, DECEMBER 23, 2010**

As the editors of the Financial Times explain, in a fast-moving non-linear market, benchmarking and traditional operational management planning models no longer work.

Why?

All you would be doing is extrapolating the status quo... a status quo that is probably already obsolete.

## Opportunity Costs in the Real World: A Case Study

**Hamdi Ulukaya**

What is the opportunity cost of accepting old, obsolete assumptions and paradigms? See for yourself.

Let's travel back in time to 2005. In the yogurt industry, Dannon, Yoplait, and Kraft are the dominant players in the U.S. Their products are specifically formulated for the U.S. consumer, who is assumed to have an unsophisticated palate and to require a lot of sweetener to cover up the natural tanginess of yogurt. The market for yogurt is rising steadily, though very slowly, as industry leaders tinker with the flavors and varieties in their existing product lines.

Enter Hamdi Ulukaya, CEO of a small cheese company in upstate New York. Ulukaya questioned the assumptions about U.S. consumer preferences. A native of Turkey, Ulukaya was raised on a different type of yogurt – creamier in texture and tangier in flavor – known as Greek-style yogurt. When Ulukaya spotted an old Kraft Foods yogurt factory for sale, he recognized the opportunity to introduce Greek-style yogurt to the U.S. market.

*Yogurt Market*

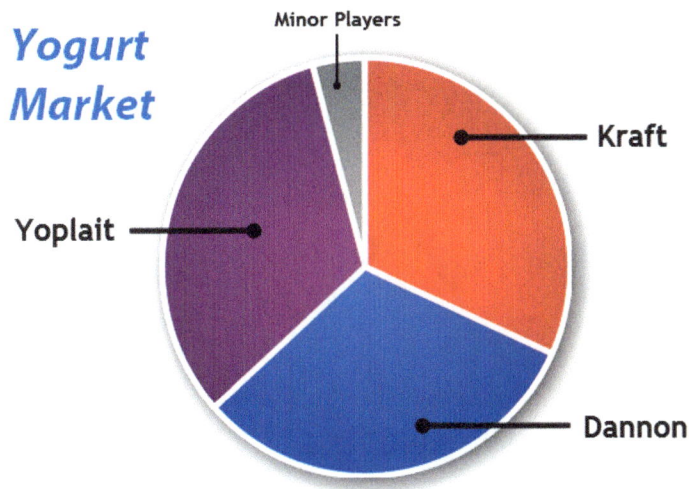

**Opportunity cost – $1 billion in sales!**

So Ulukaya bought the factory. It was challenging – financing was difficult to come by at the time – but Ulukaya had done his homework and his commitment was strong. In 2007, he introduced his Greek-style yogurt – which he called Chobani – to the U.S. consumer, starting a craze that has taken the American market by storm.

Chobani sales at startup, in 2007 – the year when the rest of the world experienced a financial crisis and the beginning of a recession: zero dollars.

Chobani sales in 2012 – just five years later: one billion dollars. That's billion with a "b," in just 2012 alone. That is equivalent to 6,200% compound annual growth, at a time when everyone else's sales were stagnant. And without a fancy pedigree or a Fortune 500 conglomerate behind him.

Why was Ulukaya able to succeed, when the rest of the world was struggling? What Ulukaya had was the ability and willingness to question outdated assumptions – and look forward rather than backward.

So consider – what would the opportunity cost have been if Ulukaya had accepted mediocrity and allowed himself to be ruled by what had worked in the past?

## $1 Billion in Sales

That is the same $1 billion opportunity that was just as available to Dannon and Kraft – if they had been willing to reject the self-fulfilling prophecy that mediocrity was destiny.

So consider... what opportunity cost are **you** paying?

## The Fork in the Road

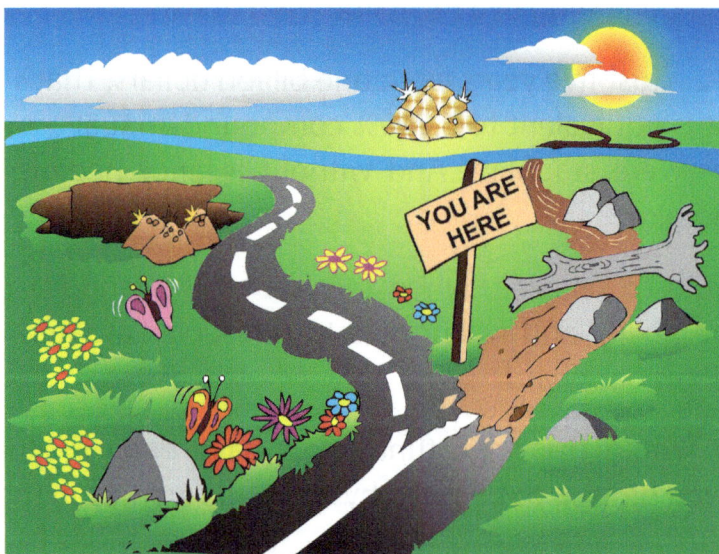

For John, like many CEOs, the choice is frighteningly clear.

He can accept the status quo – the seemingly safe but mediocre path that he is on now. But in a turbulent world, John knows that safety is an illusion. The mediocre path is actually the riskier one, because it eventually leads to a dead end. As long as John stays on the mediocre path, John's competitors are going to keep gaining on him. No matter how fast he runs, sooner or later they will overtake him, and the business he loves – the business his family and employees depend on for their livelihood – will be destroyed.

Or, John can look for a different path – a new direction that is free from the limits of outdated assumptions and self-doubts. The potential opportunity of a different path is limitless. But John is well aware that not every new path leads to greatness. Before John opts to travel outside of his comfort zone, he needs a way to reduce the risk. He needs certainty. He needs to be sure that he has put the business on the right road and that he avoids any hidden dangers along the way.

So that is John's challenge: how to find that new path in order to reach the CEO greatness that he knows is inside of him – and unearth the hidden wealth potential in his business.

**How can you be sure you are finding and
mining the hidden wealth in your business?**

**Do you share John's concerns?**

In your business: what opportunity cost are you paying – by accepting the status quo, not questioning outdated assumptions, digging in that same hole that will never yield more than meager results?

*Jay Abraham*

What risk are you running if your competitors seize the opportunity first – and get out so far ahead of you that your business can never catch up?

What processes are you following to be certain you are finding the opportunities and mining the hidden wealth lying dormant in your business?

In Part 2, we'll explore a different pathway – a new, proven leadership paradigm for creating wealth in turbulent times.

# PART 2

## The Updated Paradigm

# The Hidden Art of Foresight

Remember Hamdi Ulukaya? As he stood poised at his fork in the road, deciding whether to accept the status quo of his tiny cheese factory or strike out on a different path, which eventually led to founding Chobani, Ulukaya realized an important truth.

*Carlos Dias*

In a world of hyper-turbulent change, CEO greatness cannot be achieved by looking in the rear-view mirror.

And you certainly will not get there by standing still and waiting for outside events to decide your fate.

To achieve CEO greatness – you need to build a new skill set: you need to master the art of foresight!

**"Foresight is the ability to predict what is likely to happen – and use this information to prepare for the future."**

That is why Jay Abraham and I so strongly believe that foresight is the most important skill for a CEO today.

In our fast-moving world, foresight empowers a CEO to take advantage of opportunities that present themselves – and to avoid problems that will trap organizations that are still looking backwards.

# The Foresight Myth

Your competitors would like you to believe that foresight is an innate gift, akin to biblical prophecy. Either you were born with it, or you are out of luck.

Actually, foresight is more like athletic talent. Some of us were born with more athletic talent, and some with less. But all of us – no matter what level we begin at – can improve with practice. In fact, the highest achieving athletes are the ones who are most dedicated to refining and improving their skills. They are the ones who are always on the lookout for the best coaches, the most successful approaches – the edge that will allow them to break through to the next level of performance.

The same is true with foresight. It's a skill set that can be acquired. You can build your foresight muscles – and become that strategic, accurate-thinking CEO who can "see around corners" and prepare your organization for what is coming at you.

But, just as in athletics, it will take work. It will take dedication.

# The Need for Accurate Thinking

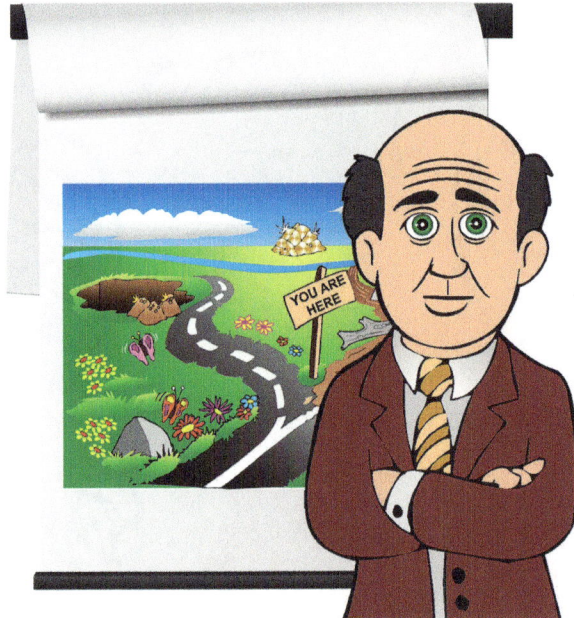

But work and dedication alone won't be enough! For our friend John – and for **you** – to develop your foresight to its fullest potential, it will also take careful, consistent, guided practice with an accurate-thinker mentor – not a tactician.

Why? Because tacticians, almost by definition, do not look forward. They tend to reason from hindsight, to make short-term decisions based either on what worked for them in the past – or worse yet, what they read about in a textbook or academic case study or benchmarking report.

*Tacticians ask: "How can we dig faster?"*

As a result, tacticians ask the wrong questions. Their focus is on working *efficiently*... on doing things right... on doing what you did yesterday but doing them better than ever before.

By contrast, accurate-thinking strategists think longer-term using foresight. Their focus is on *effectiveness* – figuring out what change is coming, so you can do the right things.

*Accurate-Thinking Strategists ask:*
*"How can we be sure we are digging in the right place?"*

Why does it matter?

Because resources are always constrained – more so than ever in turbulent times. When change is constant and fast-paced, can you see why CEOs must learn how to focus accurately and strategically on the 20% of activities that will propel their organizations forward – and avoid the 80% that are merely distracting busy-work? Can you see why CEOs must change their paradigm and master foresight?

## Focus on Creating and Capturing Value

*"While conventional wisdom would suggest a greater focus on efficiency and investments in a time of growing economic pressure, the findings of the Big Shift suggest a longer term view....*

*Today's business environment requires a focus on value creation and capture. Knowledge flows are the key to surviving and thriving through these tough times and beyond."*

**"THE 2011 SHIFT INDEX: MEASURING THE FORCES OF LONG-TERM CHANGE,"
DELOITTE CENTER FOR THE EDGE, 2011**

Accurate-thinking strategists are willing to see the fundamental truth in business today – that a "Big Shift" is occurring; a "New Normal" is emerging. The tactical orientation that worked in the twentieth century will undermine your business in the twenty-first century and eventually topple it.

Today, your focus must be on creating and capturing value. And your tools for creating and capturing value are the knowledge and know-how that you and your organization bring to the table.

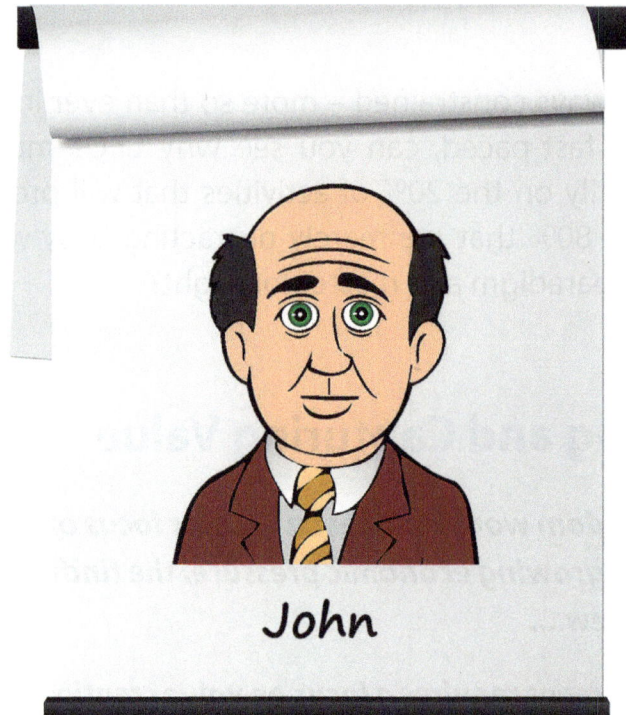

John

What about our friend John? His situation resonates with so many CEOs who are struggling today – some whose businesses are stuck and they don't even know it, others who are stuck but don't know what is causing it.

John hasn't had the luxury of standing back and taking a longer view of the situation. But if he had, here is the nature of the changes he is facing, based on research from the Shift Index:

- The performance gap between winners and losers continues to increase, with the "winners" barely maintaining previous performance levels, while losers experience rapid deterioration in performance.
- The "topple rate" of big companies has more than doubled – so previous "winners" are in danger.
- Competitive intensity in the United States has more than doubled in the last 40 years.
- Adoption of a new "digital infrastructure" is two to five times faster than adoption of previous technological infrastructures, such as electricity and the telephone.

–STEVE DENNING,
"SHIFT INDEX 2011: THE MOST IMPORTANT BUSINESS STUDY—EVER?" FORBES 1/25/12

# Technology Infrastructure Makes the Value-Chain Paradigm Obsolete

Are you wondering, if John is not running a tech company, why should the emergence of a new technology infrastructure matter to him?

It matters because – while most gurus and educators continue to teach the old value-chain concept of competitive advantage developed by Michael Porter in the 1980s – John is learning that technology has overturned and made obsolete the value-chain paradigm, causing disruption in every industry.

This disruption is affecting different industries at different speeds, but they are all affected to some degree.

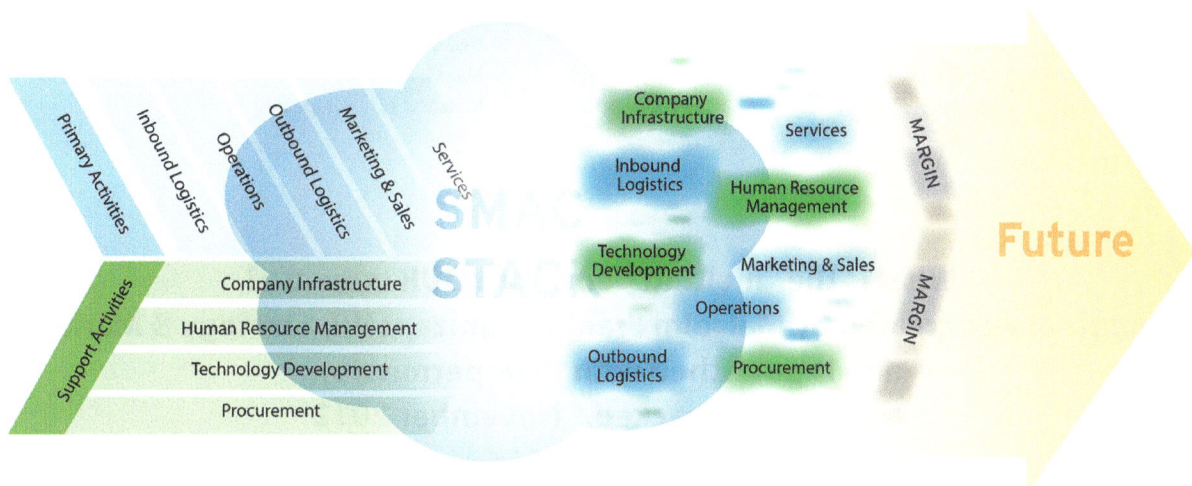

**This diagram was created by Malcolm Frank, Cognizant VP, Strategy & Marketing, and is published with their permission. "Don't Get Smacked," November 2012**

The Cognizant diagram illustrates how social, mobile, analytics, and cloud IT architecture – the "SMAC Stack" – will lead to the unbundling of tightly-coupled, industrial-age value-chains, transforming key processes and, in some cases, entire industry structures.

Different industries – like substances in nature – have different "melting points" at which this disruption will impact them. No natural substance is immune to heat – and no industry structure, including John's (and yours!), is immune to today's explosion of information.

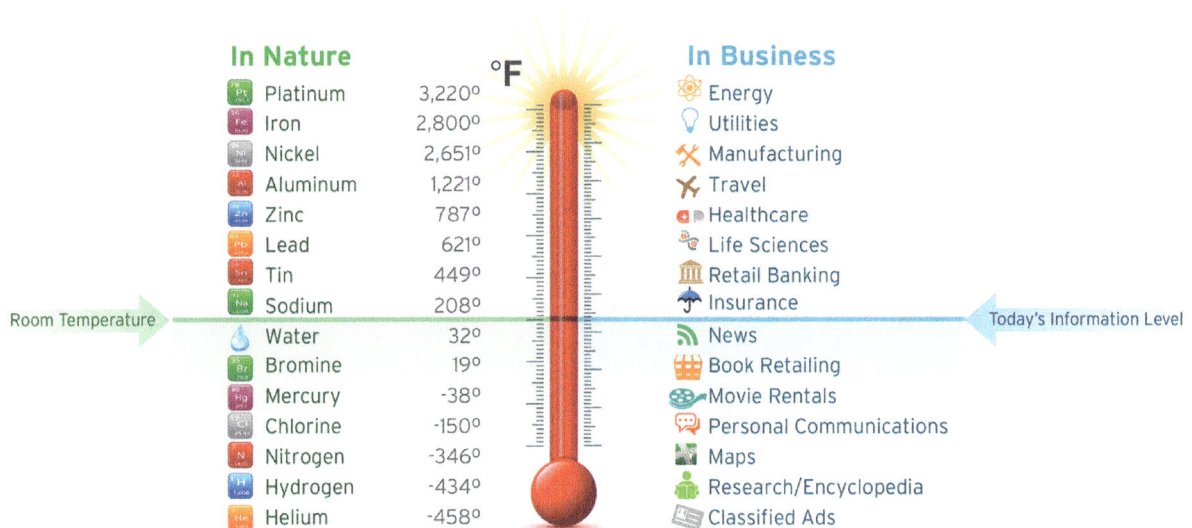

| In Nature | | | In Business |
|---|---|---|---|
| Platinum | 3,220° | | Energy |
| Iron | 2,800° | | Utilities |
| Nickel | 2,651° | | Manufacturing |
| Aluminum | 1,221° | | Travel |
| Zinc | 787° | | Healthcare |
| Lead | 621° | | Life Sciences |
| Tin | 449° | | Retail Banking |
| Sodium | 208° | | Insurance |
| Water | 32° | | News |
| Bromine | 19° | | Book Retailing |
| Mercury | -38° | | Movie Rentals |
| Chlorine | -150° | | Personal Communications |
| Nitrogen | -346° | | Maps |
| Hydrogen | -434° | | Research/Encyclopedia |
| Helium | -458° | | Classified Ads |

Room Temperature → | °F | ← Today's Information Level

**What is the "melting point" of YOUR industry?**
**This diagram was created by Malcolm Frank, Cognizant VP, Strategy & Marketing, and is published with their permission.**
**"Don't Get Smacked," November 2012[1]**

No wonder John's business is underperforming, no matter how hard he works! He is pushing on levers that are no longer connected to current economic reality.

[1]You can learn more about the SMAC Stack and its implications from: *http://www.cognizant.com*.

# How Can John Get Back on Course?

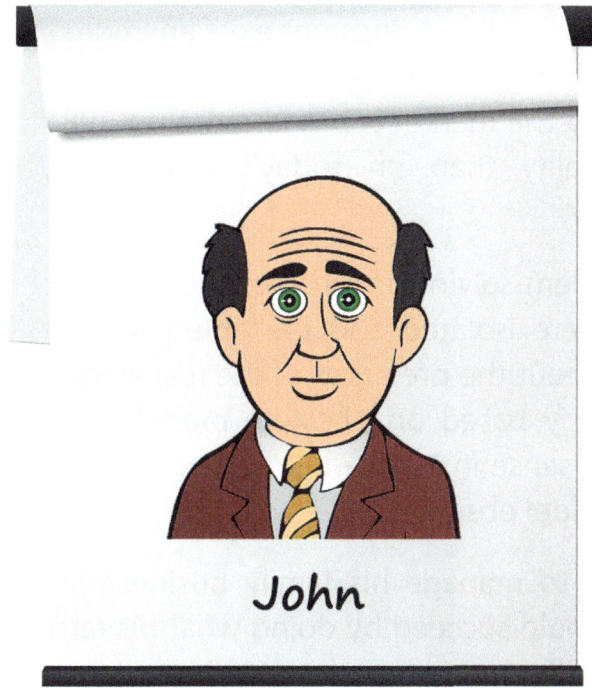

John

How can John turn his situation around while there's still time?

If you recall, John's business was under-performing. He was spending his days rushing from meeting to meeting, supervising one initiative after another in an attempt to rescue the organization. He was exhausted and stressed, and worst of all, completely confused about what to do next.

How would you advise John? Do you see a way for him to get his business back on course?

In his years as CEO of successful multinational global companies, then as mentor and coach to many other CEOs, Carlos Dias has first-hand, practical insights into cases like John's. Carlos' clients happily pay him many thousands of dollars – in fact, one client paid him over a million in just a few years – to learn from him the skills they needed to succeed profitably.

So let's see what Carlos has to say about John's situation.

Like many CEOs today, John was trained to do his job in a simpler world – a world that does not exist anymore... a world in which the value chain of activities required to deliver a product to the market is based more on 1985 Michael Porter reality than on today's unbundled, boundaryless reality.

*Carlos Dias*

John learned problem-solving in business school. But there, problems were isolated and presented to him one at a time – without the pressures of the real world. There he learned to set business strategy based on obsolete models, such as the five-forces analysis that made sense in 1979 – before the Internet, smart phones, and iPads made that model obsolete.

John learned how to manage his family business from his father – and expected that he could succeed by doing what his father had always done. But now he is in a different environment and is facing a much faster pace of change.

By trying to manage by looking backward, John – like most executives today – is wasting effort, wasting time, and burning through cash that could be used to get the business back on track.

As a result, he has allowed his business to get out of balance; his Return on Assets (ROA) is well below his cost of capital – which means he is destroying wealth when he should be building it. Worse yet, he doesn't know how to bring his situation back into balance.

If I were mentoring John, I would try to help him shift his paradigm. I would begin by asking him a simple question. I am willing to bet that he – like most CEOs today – will find this question very hard to answer.

That question is:

**"As CEO, what is your actual job description today, in turbulent times? What duties and tasks do you consider to be your unique responsibilities as the CEO of your organization?"**

# The CEO's Job Description in Turbulent Times

Carlos has found that struggling CEOs often misunderstand the fundamental purpose of their job. They realize – in fact they very much take to heart – the fact that *they* are solely responsible for their organization's success or failure.

***The CEO is responsible for the organization's success or failure.***

But what does that mean, exactly? Without a clear job description in their own minds, CEOs can easily get distracted – and neglect the core issues their organizations vitally need them to focus on.

So here is Carlos' job description for a CEO in turbulent times – the unique responsibilities of a CEO – from a man with real-world, successful, on-the-ground experience mastering that role himself.

We'll start with the CEO's duties and then drill down.

# CEO's 1st Duty: Set Strategic Direction

**Set Strategic Direction**

The first and foremost duty of the CEO, which should be performed in conjunction with your staff, is to set the organization's strategic direction.

### CEO's Duties: Set Strategic Direction

Many leaders get confused about the difference between strategy and tactics. Strategy is deciding "what" your organization should do. A CEO is paid to think – and strategy is all about accurate thinking. You, along with your key people, need to accurately assess the realities in your business environment. You need to evaluate the opportunities available to you and select the best ones to focus on – in other words, where you want your business to play and, just as importantly, where not to play. You need to conceptualize a vision of how your business can create sustainable growth and wealth in your focus areas and communicate that vision in a way that will inspire your people and align them so they can make appropriate decisions toward achieving the vision.

***Strategy happens above the shoulders.***

In other words, *strategy* is an activity that occurs above the shoulders, not below. Strategy is about effectiveness – making sure the organization is doing the right things.

### *Tactics are NOT the CEO's job!*

By contrast, *tactics* are what happens below the shoulders. It's about efficiency – doing things well. Its focus is doing rather than thinking. Tactics explain "how" the organization will accomplish its strategy. If you are spending your time writing detailed plans and spreadsheets, you are probably focusing on tactics. But that's not the CEO's job! Your people are paid to "do." You are paid to "think."

An accurate-thinking strategist CEO thinks of his or her organization as existing within an ecosystem. Your organization is the internal portion of the ecosystem. It coexists in an external ecosystem with other players – like suppliers or customers, for example. At one time, there were static hierarchies and roles within the ecosystem. For example, your office equipment vendor was the supplier and you were the customer – your roles in relation to each other did not change.

But in turbulent times, the environment is more dynamic. The entity that is your supplier today could be your customer or even your competitor tomorrow. Relationships are more fluid. CEOs who lack a strategic mindset often ignore this key fact!

## Internal and External Ecosystems

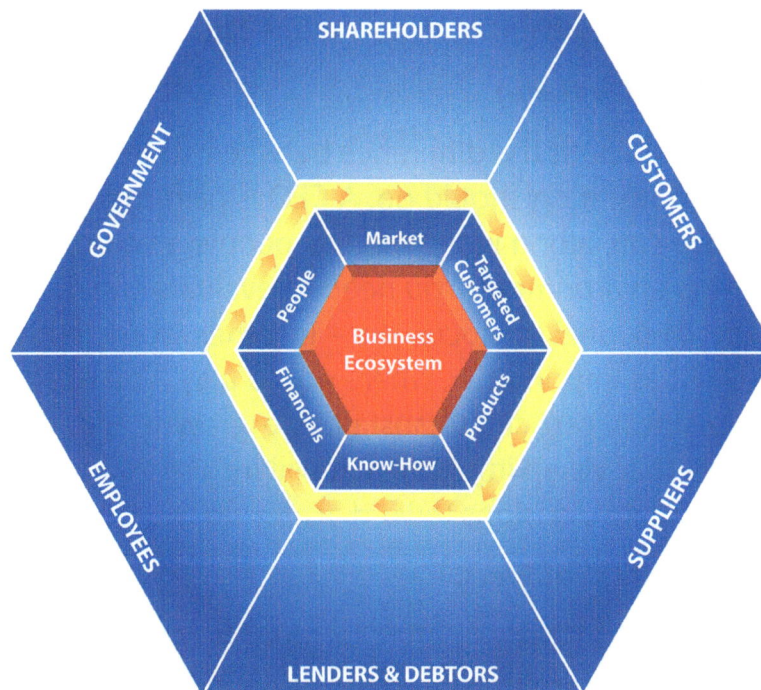

Most CEOs are familiar with the concept of an *internal* ecosystem. They are comfortable in that space. If there is a problem in their current strategy, they know how to tinker with their choice of markets, clients, products, and so forth.

But few CEOs pay attention to their *external* ecosystem. Those are the roles on the outside of the diagram. In turbulent times, a CEO needs to be mindful of the crucial strategic roles each of those external groups can play in relation to the business.

Would you like an example of why the relationship with the external ecosystem is strategically important? Let's use Apple.

In 2012, Apple had 20 Billion "app" downloads from its iTunes network. Most of these apps are not made by Apple, but they are sold through Apple's online storefront. This gives Apple a huge competitive advantage in what it can offer its customers. But to enjoy that advantage, the apps have to work well. That's why Apple demands that all of its app vendors meet stringent quality standards before they can sell apps through iTunes.

Also note that Apple commands a hefty percentage of each vendor's sale for the privilege of selling on iTunes – without having to invest in the infrastructure that would be required to create these apps if the vendors were part of Apple's internal ecosystem.

Can you see how defining the relationship with members of the external ecosystem is a core issue in Apple's strategy?

## The "Meaningful Outside"

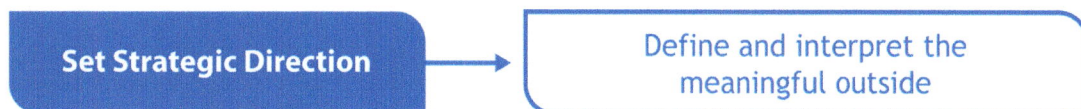

**Set Strategic Direction** → Define and interpret the meaningful outside

By the way, Apple's strategy is by no means unique. We could tell similar stories about Amazon, Google, or countless smaller and less-well-known family businesses. The principle is universal: during turbulent times, an organization's external ecosystem can provide enormous strategic leverage – for a CEO who understands its potential.

The bad news is that most CEO activity is so frenetic, so unplanned and unsynchronized, that they can't think clearly enough to see the growth potential lying latent in their ecosystem. And they similarly can't see the threat to their growth by ignoring their ecosystem's potential.

*"The CEO alone experiences the meaningful outside at an enterprise level and is responsible for understanding it, interpreting it, advocating for it, and presenting it so that the company can respond in a way that enables sustainable sales profit, and total shareholder return growth."*

**PETER F. DRUCKER**
*WALL STREET JOURNAL – DECEMBER 2004*

You see, in today's turbulent environment, where every market segment is under continuous attack by newly arriving competition, no individual business is strong enough to proactively address every possible challenge. But organizations that have developed and co-evolved their external ecosystem can form mutually beneficial relationships with customers, suppliers, even selected competitors – to defeat competitive threats and seize opportunities that would never have been available to them if they were working alone.

Can you see what Peter Drucker meant when he said, "It is up to the CEO to understand, interpret, advocate for and present the 'meaningful outside' so the business can grow and profit from it"?

Remember, the CEO's first duty is to set strategic direction for the organization. So an important task under that duty is to define and interpret that critical "meaningful outside" that Peter Drucker describes.

## Determine the "Business Backbone"

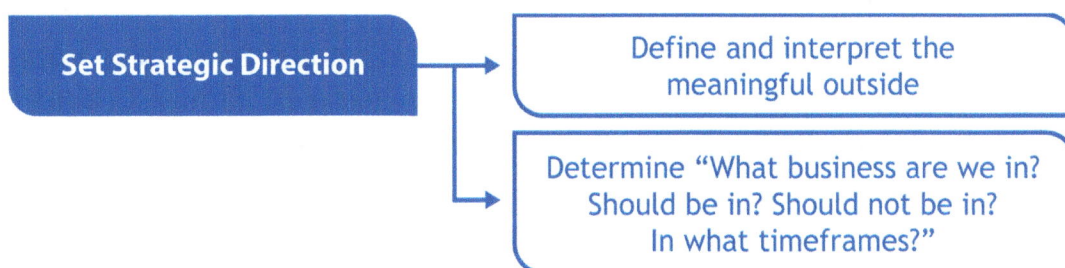

**Set Strategic Direction** → Define and interpret the meaningful outside

→ Determine "What business are we in? Should be in? Should not be in? In what timeframes?"

The next critical CEO task is determining vision, purpose, and strategic position – what Carlos calls the "business backbone" of the organization.

This is where the CEO defines:

- What game to play, and where to play it?
- Which markets and clients should we select – and which should we stay out of?
- Against which competitors?
- In which locations?
- With what product or service lines?
- And, vitally important in a fast-moving world, in what timeframes?

Would you like an example of why timing is so crucial in turbulent times? Think of Microsoft, which released a tablet computer to the market in 2013. Reviewers say it would have been a fantastic product – *if it had been released ten years ago.*

Just as it is important for the CEO to determine where and when to play, it is equally important to decide what the organization *will not* do.

Why? Especially in fast-changing times, there are never enough resources – so focus will be key to succeed in leveraging the key opportunities available for creating business wealth in a turbulent world.

So the second task under your duty to "set strategic direction" is to clearly determine and establish a strong business backbone!

### Does this sound familiar?

The reality is that most CEOs get tripped up on their business backbone because they haven't decided where to play. Instead – ask yourself if this sounds familiar – they make a list of their current competitors and then they create an operational tactic to compete against them. *In turbulent times, that is a recipe for disaster.* You end up trying to do too many things at the same time – and doing them ineffectively. The end result is stagnant sales, higher inventories, lower profits, and lower dividends – exactly what is happening with John.

# You Need Foresight in Turbulent Times!

|  | More Important | Less Important |
|---|---|---|
| **TARGETED MARKET SEGMENTS** | | |
| **TARGETED CUSTOMERS** | | |
| **TARGETED PRODUCTS** | | |
| **TARGETED GEOGRAPHICAL AREAS** | | |
| **TARGETED TIME** | 2010 | 2012 |

In turbulent times, you need the foresight to recognize new competitors coming your way. There could be new direct competitors in your field, of course. Or there could be indirect competition – new, competing claims on the customer's disposable income.

You need to know how to change your paradigm and mental models before you can either change the rules of game, or better yet, create a new game in which your organization is the leader. But first you need to have the knowledge, understanding, and wisdom – in other words, the strategic skills – to do it!

Here is where you can see the benefit of foresight-based insight. Traditional CEOs wrongly rely on their gut instinct – or on costly traditional market research. But both of those are backward-looking indicators. It isn't possible for them to turn up indirect trends before they happen. That is why CEOs with foresight have developed new ways of spotting oncoming trends – ways that are more forward-looking than listening to what your gut tells you – ways that are more applicable in a new, fast-moving world.

*So think about it.* If you can spot indirect competition while it is still "around the corner," you will have a huge competitive advantage, won't you? Can you see how foresight-based insight will strengthen your business's strategic hand?

Peter Drucker said it best:

**"The greatest danger in times of turbulence is not the turbulence itself. It is acting with yesterday's logic, basing your actions only on past experiences."**

**PETER DRUCKER**

## Allocate Human and Financial Resources

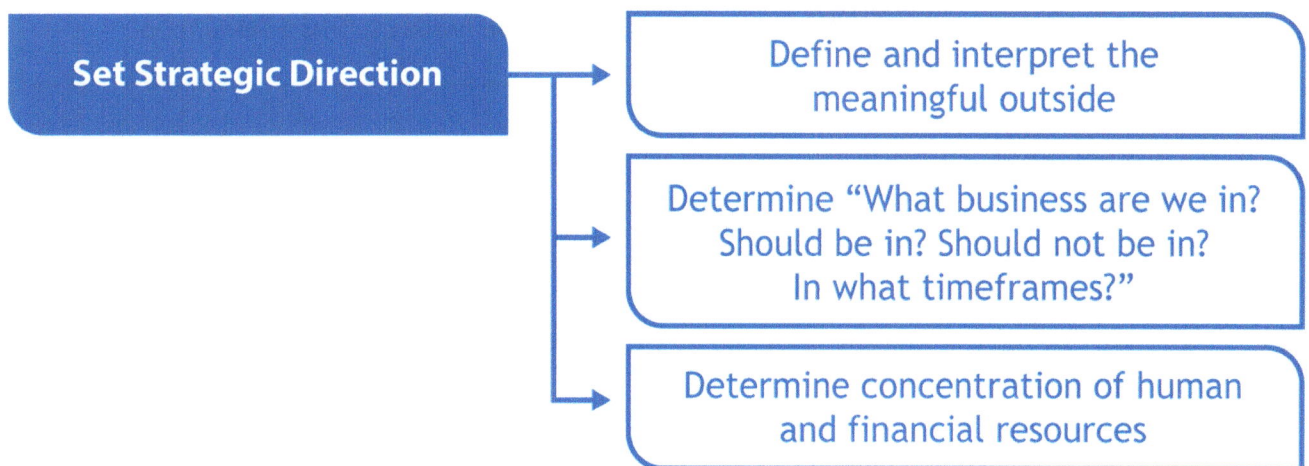

**Set Strategic Direction**

→ Define and interpret the meaningful outside

→ Determine "What business are we in? Should be in? Should not be in? In what timeframes?"

→ Determine concentration of human and financial resources

There is one more dimension to the CEO's strategic duties: deciding how to allocate human and financial resources in order to carry out the strategy.

In turbulent times, the two scarcest resources are *talented humans* with proven capacity to understand where the market is headed – and *financial capital* that allows you to invest in pursuing the opportunities in your business.

It is up to the CEO to determine the answer to questions like: What is the best way to put our most talented people to work for us? How much of our profit do we need to reinvest in the business and how much should we distribute to the owners?

These are hard choices, but vital ones if the business is going to grow in turbulent times.

To sum up, the CEO's first duty is to set strategic direction. That includes:

- Defining and interpreting the meaningful outside
- Determining "What business are we in? Should be in? Should not be in? In what timeframes?"
- Determining concentration of human and financial resources

## CEO's 2nd Duty: Set the Cultural Tone

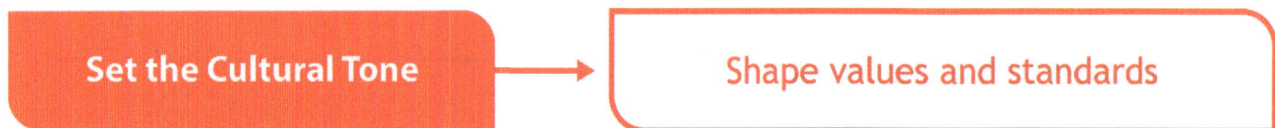

Set the Cultural Tone → Shape values and standards

Duty #2 of the CEO is to build the organization's culture – the customs and beliefs and mental models – the way of life and social interactions among all members. Culture is a tough concept because it is hard to see. Culture is actually the meaning that the people in your organization attach to their actions. You can't see the meaning – but you can see the collective behavior of the people who make up your organization, and your customers can see it too!

***Values tell you what is important to the organization!***

That is why **defining the organization's values** is so vital. Values tell you what is important to the organization… what is it like to work in it… do business with it… live on the same planet with it. The CEO must define these cultural imperatives and then find a way to communicate them so they can be interpreted consistently throughout the organization.

Why? Without leadership, people – like organizations – move too slowly and without clear direction. Without leadership, they lose their way – and the organization never gets anywhere.

# Values Are About Behavior

*"In the absence of explicitly defined standards, people will develop their own; that's human nature.*

*"Unfortunately, this lack of explicit standards is common in organizations today. Under these conditions, how can you expect your organization to become a leader in your market?"*

**CARLOS DIAS**

Your organization's purpose or standards are the measuring sticks for values. They are how your people know if they are behaving in a way that is in keeping with the organization's values. These are the mile-markers you lay down to lead your people, so they know they are staying on the right path.

Most CEOs think values should be left to their Human Resources department, but they are wrong. Values have strategic importance. Your values establish your identity in the minds of your customers. For example, think about how Hewlett Packard is viewed by today's marketplace. Their CEO failed to control the values of the organization. Over time, their values evolved to implicitly place the employees' needs ahead of the consumers. The result was mismanagement, lack of effectiveness, and a record of wrong decisions.

Would you like examples? How about when Hewlett Packard's board fired three CEOs in less than five years, without recognizing their own fault in selecting people unprepared to lead the company? Or when HP invested over $10 billion to acquire a new company, then admitted only one year later that they were wrong – and of course writing-off the investment in their balance sheet.

### You can learn a lot from others' wrong decisions

There are lessons here for any company, of any size, in any industry. One lesson is about what a lack of over-arching values can represent in terms of business performance – in wasted opportunity, in lower dividends, and in some cases, eventually even in business bankruptcy. For a CEO, *it is imperative to understand the lessons and connect the dots – to see how the leadership values that guide you and your organization impact the lives of so many people whose fortunes are tied to yours.*

Establishing corporate values could and should be a positive weapon in the CEO's arsenal. *In turbulent times, the CEO can use values and standards strategically*, as a way to move the organization forward, helping people to understand the meaning behind their actions. How? By taking the lead in setting ethical standards that are in keeping with an overall identity that will define the organization in the minds of the public. In other words, *your values can be your brand.*

## CEO's 3rd Duty: Build the Organizational Team

| Build the Organizational Team | → | Team building |
|---|---|---|

Duty #3 in our job description is team building. Why is this the CEO's job?

Here's why, in the words of Walter Wriston, the Citibank CEO who is widely regarded as the most influential commercial banker of his time.

*"The person who figures out how to harness the collective genius of his or her organization is going to blow the competition away."*

**WALTER WRISTON**
*CITIBANK CEO (1967-1984)*

As Wriston explains, any CEO who can align the heads, hearts, and hands of employees will create an unstoppable force in the marketplace.

Here is another way to look at it, from the Swiss think tank, the Gottlieb Duttweiler Foundation.

*"Only 20% of the knowledge available to an organization is actually used."*

**GOTTLIEB DUTTWEILER FOUNDATION**

Intellectual capital in most organizations is being wasted. Knowledge, wisdom, and understanding can be an invaluable resource for competitive advantage. Finding a way to harness the value of intellectual capital is likely to be one of the preeminent challenges of twenty-first century business leaders.

It starts with harnessing the intellectual capital of the executive team. That's why only the CEO should be able to hire and lead senior management. Only the CEO should be able to fire non-performers on the senior management team. It needs to be the CEO's team – because, remember, success or failure is ultimately the CEO's responsibility.

## Final Words

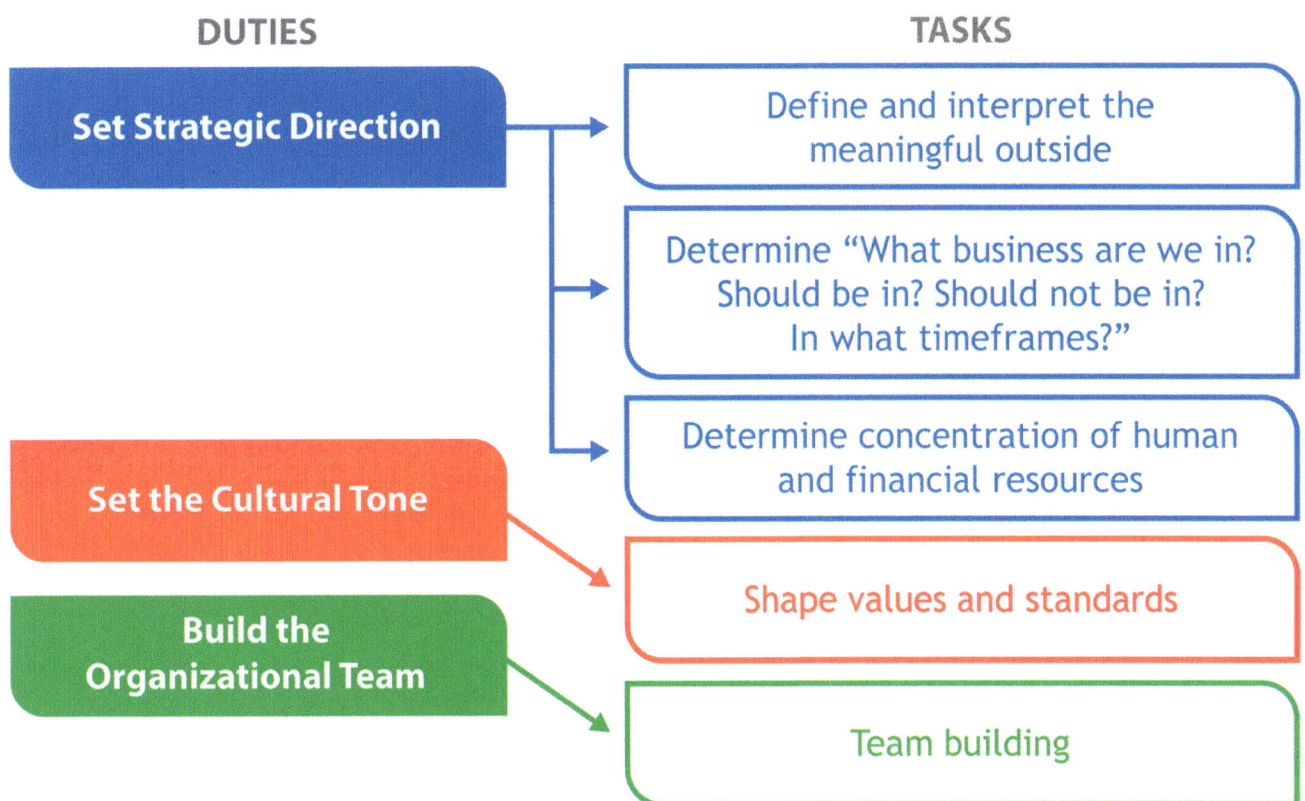

Were you surprised by Carlos' CEO job description for turbulent times – either by the duties and tasks that are on the list, or the ones that aren't on the list?

Many CEOs are shocked – because it is quite different from their own mental models. That's the point. In turbulent times, if you want to achieve CEO greatness, you are going to need to find a way to reshape your mental model – to shift your paradigm – and face the realities of being a CEO in the twenty-first century.

*Jay Abraham*

**Before you can be great, you need to be different**. That applies to you, the CEO, and your senior executives as well.

- You need to get effective and efficient, so you can outperform the competition again and again, even in turbulent times.
- You need to become an accurate thinker. Having acuity means being able to think, see, and hear clearly, to be able to see the true facts that make up your reality, rather than things that have been guessed-at or made up.

It's only then that you will achieve greatness.

**"People and their organizations cannot achieve greatness for the simple reason that they don't have an idea, a picture, in their mind's eye of what greatness looks like."**

Let's talk about greatness.

I believe – in fact, I have based my life's work on – the ability of each of us to achieve greatness in whatever we do. We're programmed for it.

No one – not me, not you, not John – says, "My life's goal is to be mediocre." We all want to achieve something spectacular.

So why doesn't it happen?

Read on.

# Barriers to Greatness

First, most people don't have a good picture in their mind's eye of what greatness is for them. John wants to be a great CEO – but he doesn't have a vision in his mind of what that could mean, either for him or for his business. It's impossible to get there if you can't describe where "there" is.

***You need a vision of what "greatness" is for YOU.***

Second, even if people have the vision, they have no idea how to achieve it. Mediocrity is easy – that's the path that everyone takes, so just follow the crowd and you are sure to get there. Greatness is harder – you'll need to find a different path from the rest of the herd if you are going to get there.

***You need a PATH to take you there.***

Third, you need to be committed. Greatness isn't about taking one step and then quitting. Greatness is achieved by taking the first step, then the next, and then the next. Greatness requires a promise to yourself to do and to behave in a particular way; in other words, the willingness to work smarter and give your energy and time to become an accurate-thinker leader.

***You need COMMITMENT.***

Underlying all of this is courage and self-confidence. You need to develop your belief that your vision is the right one. You have to know in your heart that you have the right roadmap to get there, the commitment to adjust your roadmap if any barriers spring up to stop you, and the courage to adjust your paradigm and acquire the new skills you will need to lead in the twenty-first century.

***You need COURAGE and SELF-CONFIDENCE.***

So consider this... do you think our friend John can achieve greatness?

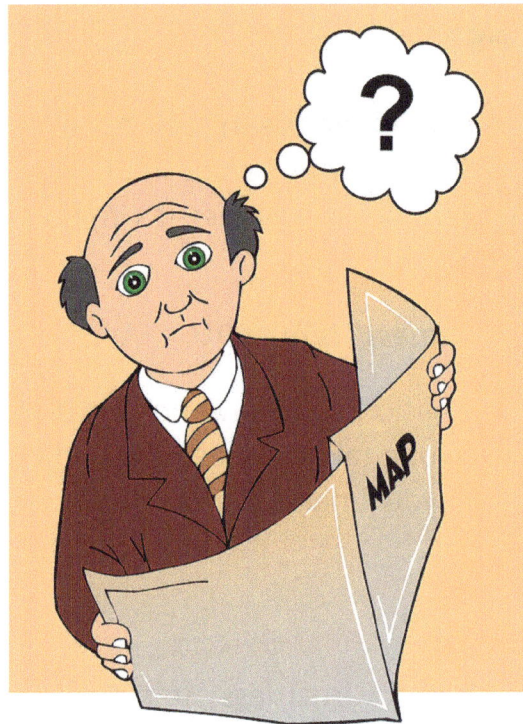

We have already learned how mediocrity is working out for John. But what would achieving CEO greatness do for him?

- If John could *strengthen his foresight*, he could envision his business as an engine for breakthrough, sustainable, profitable growth – maybe a one billion dollar company instead of a 300 million dollar one – doubling or tripling his profits and the dividends his family can enjoy.

- If John could *shift his paradigm* about his job as CEO in a global marketplace that is undergoing unprecedented disruption, he could chart a new path to accomplish his vision – a new path that will let his organization double or triple the return on assets (ROA). In other words, John would be creating true wealth… and funding larger dividends for his family and shareholders!

- If John could muster the commitment, courage, and self-confidence required to *inspire himself and his stakeholders*, **John could become the great leader of a great organization**.

Greatness for John means unearthing the hidden wealth available in his business. Along the way, a transformation will happen for John… it always does… because the path to CEO greatness leads also to peace of mind – the satisfaction that you have done everything it takes to reach full potential for yourself and your business.

***CEO greatness leads also to peace of mind.***

Okay, that's inspiring. But don't kid yourself; getting to greatness is not easy. It is possible to reach CEO greatness on your own, through sheer determination, force of will, and good brainpower.

But there is another way. It's not a shortcut exactly – but it is a surer route: a hidden map that is proven to get you where you want to go.

You'll learn more about that in Part 3 of the program.

# PART 3

## The Secret Map

The last time we saw John, he was just beginning to reconnect with his potential for greatness.

Like most CEOs, John would like to think of himself as a smart, successful business person.

*Carlos Dias*

In fact, he got so excited by some of Jay's and my ideas that he even allowed himself to daydream about a vision for himself...

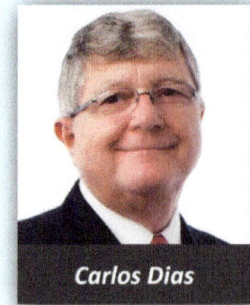

In John's daydream, he is widely respected and acknowledged for his foresight-based insight and his leadership thinking. In his daydream, his business is known as an agile, innovative market leader. Best of all, in his daydream John hasn't just grown his business – he's transformed it into a sustainable, highly-profitable legacy for his family and shareholders, well into the future.

It's a great vision.

But when John pulls out a piece of paper and tries to map out how to make it happen, he realizes that something is missing.

John doesn't know what to do next. He knows he is supposed to change – but to what? He isn't sure what the first step should be or the step after that.

How will John know what to do?

John knows that standing still and staying mediocre isn't really an option. He is willing and eager to do what it takes to change. But he can't afford to try and fail. His business can't afford rookie mistakes. He needs to know with certainty that he is on the right path before he sets out.

In this part of the program, Jay and I will show John – and you – the secret map to greatness.

# The Path to Profitability

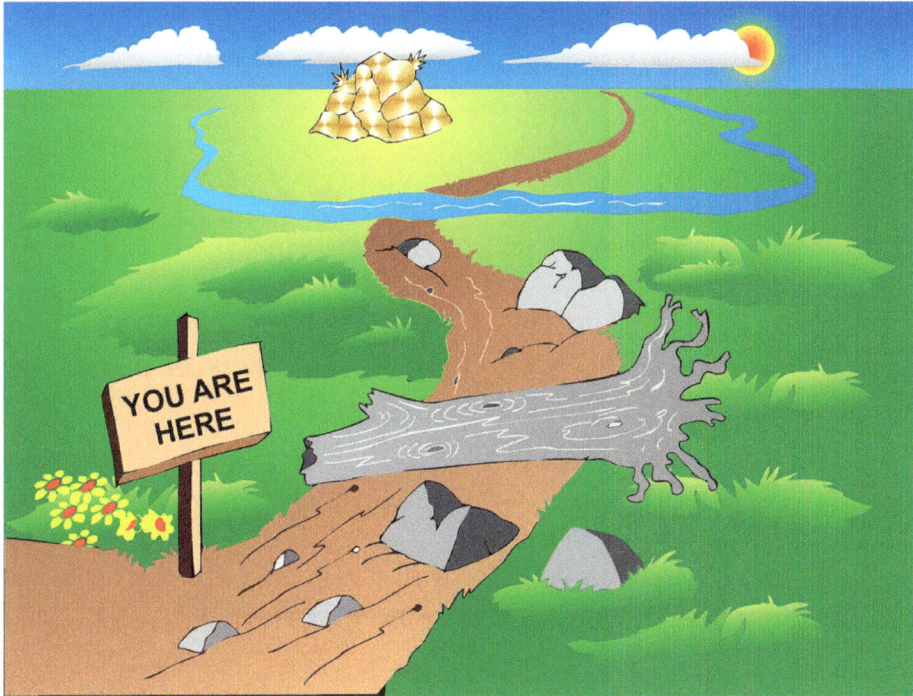

So many CEOs these days feel that sense of uncertainty. They used to feel they knew how to run their businesses. Maybe they learned how as they were growing up, maybe they learned it in business school, or maybe a little of both. It was almost like the path to profits had been laid out for them, and all they had to do was stay on it.

But somewhere along the line, the landscape seems to have shifted. The path to profitability isn't so clear anymore. They know they have to create a new path – but they don't know how.

### *Your Choice: Reality or Denial*

So many CEOs today are talkers or wishful thinkers, in denial. Wishful thinking seems to be growing in popularity today, practiced by CEOs and government leaders, particularly in the Western world. We've developed a chart that reflects data from a number of global surveys done by prestigious organizations quoted in Carlos and Jay's book *The CEO Who Sees around Corners*. These survey results match Jay and Carlos' first-hand impressions from working with CEOs and senior executives around the world.

# Grow Your Leadership Mindset

### Grow Your Leadership Mindset
#### Take a Quantum Leap to Manifest Your Leadership Potential

Growth Mindset (Modesty)

Levels of Knowledge

Greatness

Enlightened Accurate Creative Thinker

Fifth Stage: **Confidence** **5%**

Creative **Leadership** FOR TURBULENT TIMES *with Jay Abraham and Carlos Dias*

Accurate Thinker

Fourth Stage: **Trust** **5%**

Corporate Effective Strategist

● **Inflection Point** (Point Of Leverage)

Third Stage: **Wisdom** **5%**

Efficient Tactician Entrepreneur

Second Stage: **Knowledge** **50%**

Cognitive Dissonance

Denial

First Stage: **Wishful Thinking** **35%**

Low Mindset (Arrogance)

Talkers    Doers    Thinkers

Journey to Leadership

Of course, you have the right to and can refuse to see reality. But what you can never avoid is suffering the consequences of denying reality. It's like the law of gravity, a natural law that no human can change.

In fact, it's harder and more difficult to be in denial than to face reality. Denial makes you feel depressed and anxious, because in your gut you know you are a wishful thinker. You expend so much energy telling yourself stories and hiding from the truth – it's exhausting.

### *Seeing the true reality creates excitement, passion, and enthusiasm!*

Seeing the true reality, by contrast, is a very different game. It liberates your spirit. Seeing true reality creates excitement, passion, and enthusiasm. Even if it's a difficult reality, facing it makes you feel more free. Why? Because, you know the true situation and the problem, as opposed to how you would like things to be. And because now, finally, you can prepare to take action, to commit to a new direction and to acquiring new knowledge and new skills.

# Denial Leads to Arrogance

Here is what Carlos has to say about denial:

*"Denial makes you more arrogant. Every time. And arrogance leads to trouble, in your life and in your business. Every time, always! That is reality!"*

**CARLOS DIAS**

As Carlos explains, the problem with denial is that it leads to arrogance. Arrogance is a natural defense mechanism you adopt as a way to hide from true reality.

But arrogance gets you into trouble – in your private life and in your business life.

We live in times of hyper-turbulent change. It is in your own interest to accept this reality, and the implications of that reality, in contrast to what you would *like* reality to be.

You may not want to hear it, but reality is telling you that *knowledge is changing at breakneck speed*.

Look at this chart and consider its implications. In some industries, what you know to be true today will be completely obsolete in just five years. In other industries, the pace is a little slower, but the change is still undeniable. That is the reality!

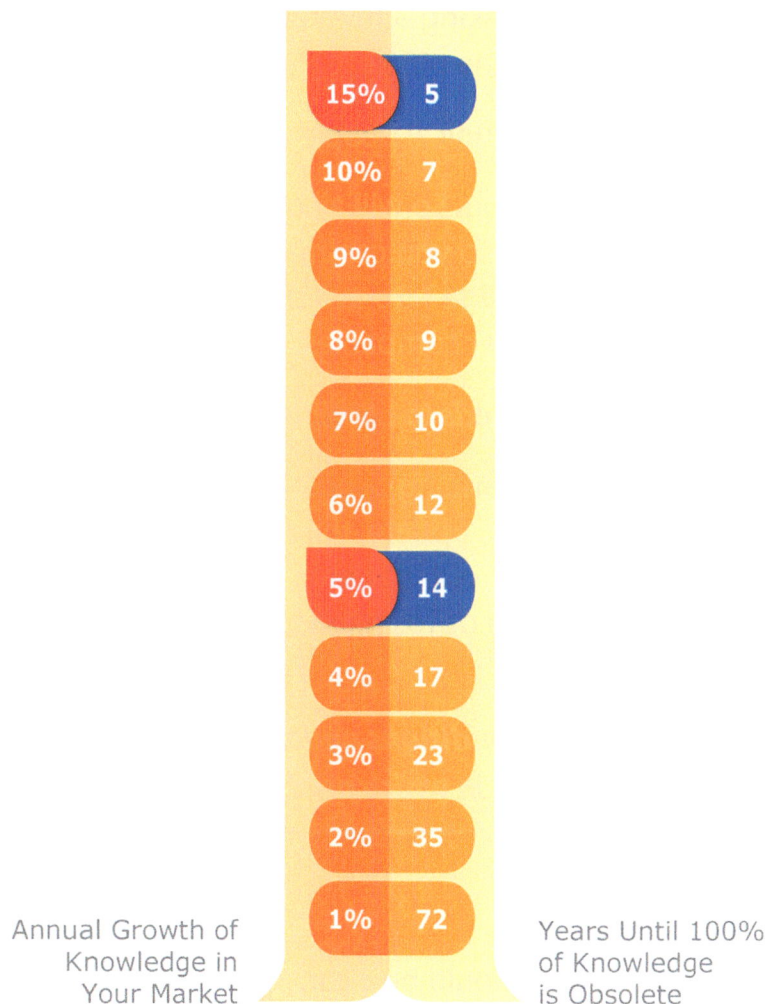

| Annual Growth of Knowledge in Your Market | Years Until 100% of Knowledge is Obsolete |
|---|---|
| 15% | 5 |
| 10% | 7 |
| 9% | 8 |
| 8% | 9 |
| 7% | 10 |
| 6% | 12 |
| 5% | 14 |
| 4% | 17 |
| 3% | 23 |
| 2% | 35 |
| 1% | 72 |

# When Knowledge Becomes Obsolete

*"Learning how to drive an automobile does not equip one to pilot a space vehicle.*
*"Knowing how to work a slide rule does not equip one to operate a computer."*

**RUSSELL ACKOFF**

What does it mean when knowledge becomes obsolete?

If you are making a mental note to tell your technical people to stay on top of this, you are missing the point!

Yes, your technical people will need to continuously update their knowledge.

But so will you. So will all of your senior executives. So will your Board. All of you need to stay current so you can make the right decisions in a fast-moving world. All of you need new knowledge – to avoid the fate of Kodak, Hewlett Packard, Circuit City, Borders, and so many other companies.

**Everyone needs to continuously update their knowledge!**

In a fast-changing world, the reality is that everyone in the organization needs to continuously update their knowledge. It's mandatory these days – it's no longer an option. The old patterns have been disrupted. The way you are managing today therefore needs to change.

*"The only conditions under which experience is the best teacher*
*are the ones in which no change takes place."*

**RUSSELL ACKOFF**

By now, it should be clear:

You need a new skill set – and so does the rest of your organization, one that can adapt to a more turbulent world.

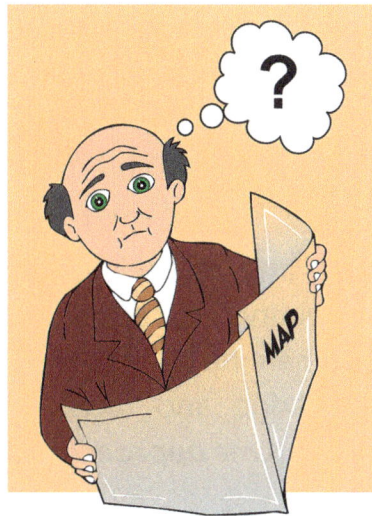

**But what skill set do you need?**

What is that skill set? What knowledge does a CEO like John need – today and tomorrow and the next day – to achieve greatness for himself and his business, to find the hidden wealth in his business – even in turbulent times like these?

## Updating Your Paradigm

Before anything else, John desperately needs to update his paradigms and mental models. He is still operating like a mid-twentieth century, tactics-oriented manager – tinkering with this idea or that, focusing on short-term outcomes, making changes to one silo at a time, and benchmarking leaders in his market. That worked fine in a slower, simpler world – where you could count on yesterday's knowledge to still be true today.

But today's world is more dynamic – and infinitely more complex. To succeed in today's turbulence, John must become a twenty-first century, accurate strategic thinker. That is the only route that will get him to where he needs to go. John needs to become a leader with foresight – based on knowledge and facts, rather than fantasies and false assumptions. He needs to **adopt a systems approach** – not just to his business, but to his personal self-development as well.

John needs to understand the effect of each of his strategic moves. The real world is not like those case studies in business school. In the real world, John will not be operating in a vacuum. So he needs to understand how different key components of his business connect up and affect one another.

## What Is Missing?

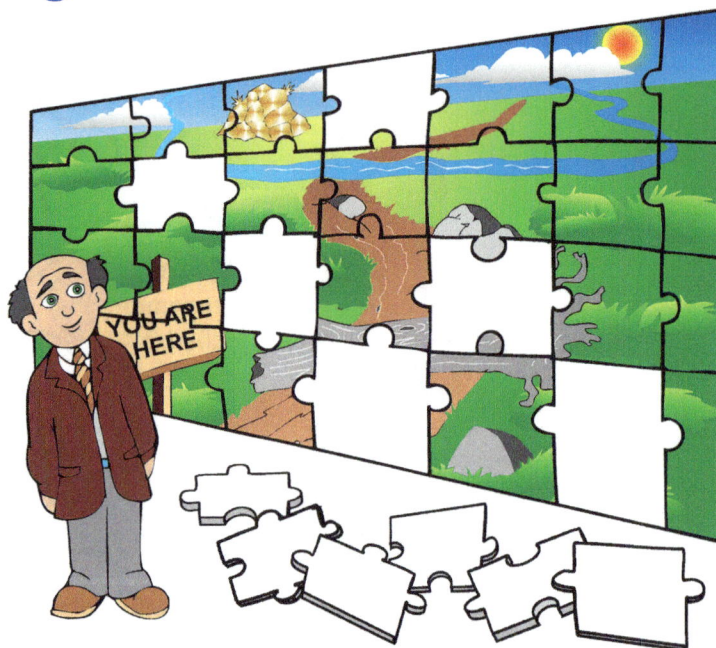

It's a different mindset – one that will require John to add some important missing pieces to his leadership approach.

*"Strategy development is the most important leadership competency, both today and in the future, and just 4 percent of CEOs fall into the strategist category."*

**AMERICAN MANAGEMENT ASSOCIATION**
*"A GLOBAL STUDY OF LEADERSHIP (2005-2015)"*

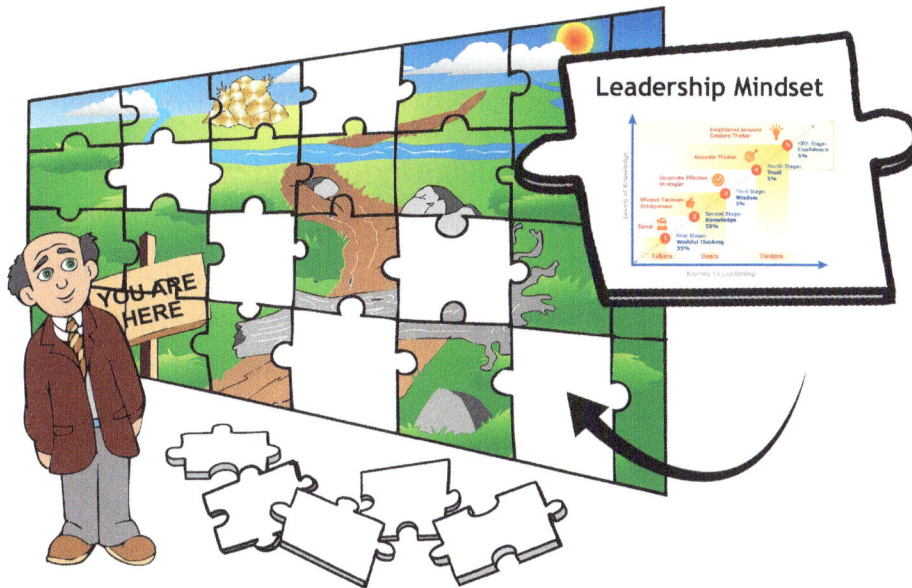

To become a highly admired, twenty-first century-ready CEO – to achieve business greatness – John needs to update his paradigm and mental models. He needs to learn how to become an enlightened creative thinking leader. It's not surprising that John lacks the know-how for this – it's a shortcoming that he shares with the preponderance of senior executives today.

But **to succeed in a complex world, John and his staff must learn to master this new, more strategic way of thinking**. John can't focus on short-term, operational issues any more. He has a new job description – so he needs a new skill set to lead in turbulent times.

John needs to learn how to craft visions that can be shared across the different action logics in his organization. His visions must be capable of encouraging both personal and organizational transformation. They must inspire the creation of new, powerful competitive strategies – and the meticulous execution of these strategies. It's not easy. John will need to practice and rehearse this new way of thinking over and over in order to master it. But **true**

**mastery can only be accomplished through a rigorous step-by-step thinking process, not just theory alone**. Why? Because even with powerful, proven concepts, we only truly learn to use them experientially – by trying, making mistakes, identifying and correcting those mistakes, and getting stronger with each iteration of the process.

# Skill Set Checklist

Here is Carlos' list of the required skill set for a twenty-first century leader:

- First and foremost, see the true reality. Understand where the business is today, why it is or is not making money, and what his strengths and weaknesses are.
- Develop the foresight to spot trends that can become opportunities or threats.
- Understand the internal and external, connected ecosystem in which the business is situated, in order to identify areas of leverage and opportunity that your competitors are missing.
- Create a business backbone – where to play and where not play – that lets you play to win, strategically selecting the customers and markets you want to be in, and which you do not.
- Define value from your customer's perspective – what they need today and what they will want tomorrow.
- Create a unique business model and singular strategy for delivering value to your customer – and capturing wealth.
- Deliver a continuous stream of innovative products within that business model and singular strategy.
- Position your sales and marketing people to thrive in a dynamic, changing marketplace.
- Get your people and processes aligned so the organization can respond quickly to new developments.
- Finally, wean yourself away from arrogance and learn to manage more collaboratively. Why? If you are going to succeed in implementing any of these other skills, you need to learn how to harvest the collective knowledge in your organization and leverage it – so you can be confident that your strategies are correct and accurate.

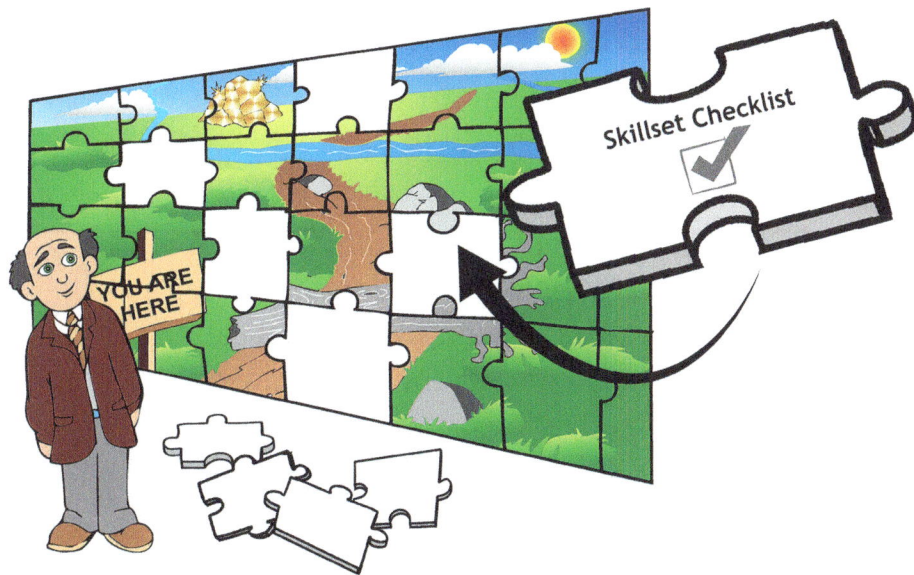

This is the skill set that you will need, the skill set of a twenty-first century creative, accurate thinker strategist, in order to lead your organization to find the hidden wealth and greatness in your organization.

Take a few moments to review each one of these requirements and ask yourself the key question: Am I what is needed to succeed in turbulent times? The answer will tell you if your organization is headed to the path of success… or destruction, and what immediate action you need to take!

**Do YOU have the skill set to succeed in turbulent times?**

How did you rate yourself on the checklist? Do you have the skills for twenty-first century leadership?

There are so many new skills, strategies, and ways of thinking! But in turbulent times, you must adapt to survive. Work smarter, work differently, and work in breakthrough ways.

Consider this quote from Peter Drucker:

*"Business is a permanent 'white paper' condition (chaos, either random or lawful), but with the added complexity of human freedom. You must therefore change: work smarter, not just harder, work differently, not just better, work in breakthrough ways, not just incrementally. The solution is to develop a leadership mind. Leadership means greatness in all you do."*

**PETER KOESTENBAUM, "LEADERSHIP: THE INNER SIDE OF GREATNESS: A PHILOSOPHY FOR LEADERS," JASSEY-BASS 2002**

# Perspectives from Carlos Dias

As a CEO myself, I know what you are thinking, because at one time in my career I was like you. You want to learn and change – but you also need to be practical. Studying for its own sake is a luxury for the school-aged. You probably wish you had appreciated that luxury more when you were back at college, but those days are gone. What you need now is to learn real-world skills that you can apply right away, in your real-world business, and you need a way to make those skills viral – to spread them through your executive team, key managers, and junior executives too – all the future leaders of your organization.

*Carlos Dias*

You need to learn all this. But you can't just take off a few weeks or years and go back to school – even if you could find a school that teaches the skills on the checklist. You won't find it in one of those week-long management seminars – you probably already have plenty of fancy binders from those seminars in your library, collecting dust.

As a practical matter, you need to do more than just learn. You need a step-by-step, real-world grounded thinking process. Theories and concepts alone are nice, but by themselves they won't make your business grow.

**You need real-world, practical processes to guide you.**

What you really need are practical processes that guide you, step-by-step, as you implement your vision. You need to learn how to use your new knowledge – and use it in a holistic way – looking at your entire ecosystem to diagnose causes, rather than just symptoms or consequences of your problems. You need to know how to act so that you make a positive difference – not just a quick fix here and a tweak over there, resulting in no real change.

I agree – the checklist of skills for twenty-first century leaders, and the job description for a twenty-first century CEO, are useful, but they are really just a menu of items that you need to learn. They laid out the big picture so you could see the holes in your current knowledge – and hopefully see the urgency of plugging those holes.

What you need now is a path for how to put all of these skills and tasks together into a new model of leadership – a system of integrated, step-by-step, proven processes – a pathway for learning how-to, as well as a pathway for doing – that you can follow in real time as you grow your company.

Jay Abraham and I have put such a system together – we call it The Strategic Wealth Creator System™.

We have proven that it works in industry after industry, country after country. **That's why we know it can work for you, too!** By working with high-performance businesses within their ecosystems, we have gained insights into what makes organizations truly distinctive, and why distinctive skills are critical to lasting competitive advantage.

We also saw how high performers successfully create and lead the unique sets of business processes and resources that support their distinctive capabilities. Six strategic divergent thinking processes make all the difference. No one process alone can give an organization a distinctive capability. Together, however, these six processes create a powerful system, the Strategic Wealth Creator System™, consistently making a real and lasting difference in company performance.

Next, we'll look at each process in the Strategic Wealth Creator System™.

# The Strategic Wealth Creator System™

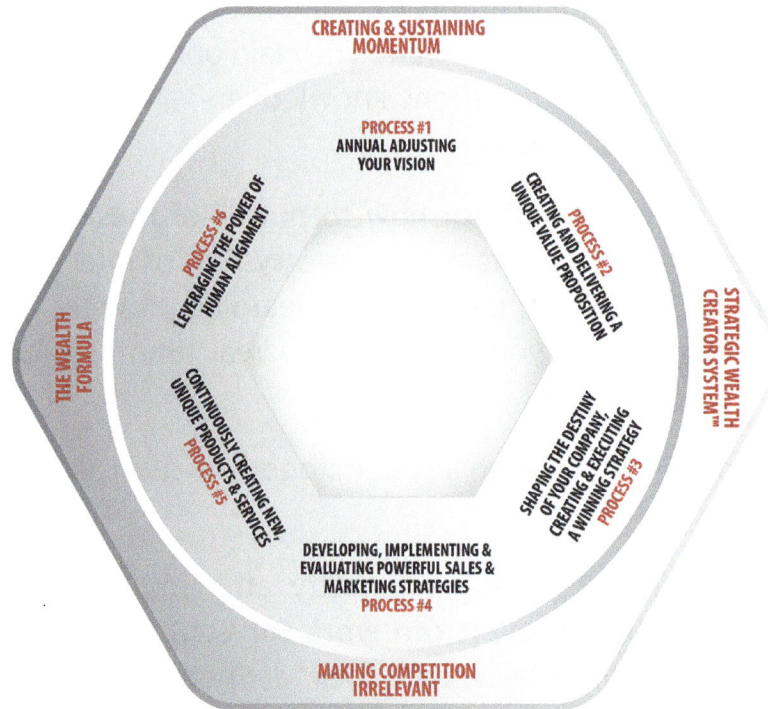

Here is how the Strategic Wealth Creator System™ works.

***Where are we headed?***
***Where should we go?***

In **strategic-thinking process #1**, you adjust your vision so you can clearly see the reality for your business from multiple perspectives. You look at the business' numbers in a new way, to see once and for all whether your current strategies are creating wealth for you – or losing it. You identify, using an exclusive proprietary process called the Web TrendWatcher™, those trends that are most likely to impact your business – for better or worse – over the next few years. You examine your current business ecosystem – both internal and external – to identify threats and opportunities. You identify bottlenecks, constraints, and frictions that prevent your organization from growing profitably. Then you put it all together into an integrated scan of your business, so you can identify the highest-priority initiatives to work on over the next few years. We promise you, by the time you complete just this one process, you will have a much deeper understanding of your business – and you will be generating exciting, innovative ideas for how to move forward!

*What do our customers really want and need?*
*Where should we go?*

In **strategic-thinking process #2**, you will swing your attention to creating a unique client value proposition. You will apply Jay Abraham's Strategy of Preeminence to become the most trusted player in your market. You'll define what "customer value" really means – and begin to understand your customers' behavior in a deeper, more meaningful way. You will plot an electronic value map for your market, so you can see instantly where you are positioned, where your competition is positioned, and – most importantly – where there are unmet customer needs and pockets of value for you to exploit. By the end of this process, you will be able to craft a unique client value proposition that accurately pinpoints what your customers really need today – and what they will want tomorrow but don't yet know. This is where you lay the foundation to succeed in a turbulent, fast-changing world.

*How can we create unique value?*
*How can we make a profit?*

In **strategic-thinking process #3**, you shape the destiny of your organization – today and into the future – by crafting a unique business model that creates unique value for your customer. You create a singular competitive strategy that puts you at a sustainable competitive advantage, so you can realistically charge more for your products and capture that wealth for your business.

*How do we achieve marketing precision*
*and sales to focus?*

As we all know, just because you build it, they won't necessarily come. So in **strategic-thinking process #4**, you implement a strategic, innovative sales process called "Laser Sales" – based on Jay Abraham's Theory of Optimization or Three Ways to Grow a Business. By the end of this process, you'll integrate the activities of your sales force, marketing programs, Web site, and all of the other ways you communicate with your customers in an exciting, consistent way. You will also learn to implement the "Performance Enhancement Quotient" developed by Jay Abraham over the last twenty years. This process virtually guarantees higher overall performance levels, capabilities, and sales results throughout a company's entire selling system. When you put these Laser Sales and the Performance Enhancement Quotient into place together, you get geometric gains and exponential improvements.

*How can we elevate "Perceived Customer Value"
to an unrivaled high?*

In **strategic-thinking process #5**, you deal with value innovation. You learn how to stay ahead of trends, maintain customer loyalty, and keep the competition at bay, by releasing a continuous stream of innovative, irresistible new products. In fact, after continually applying this process in your organization you should be able to make 30% of your annual sales with new products or services alone. Can you imagine what this could represent in terms of sustainable profits and future growing dividends for your organization?

*How do we energize and continuously
realign our organization?*

And finally, in **strategic-thinking process #6**, you crack the Genetic Code of your organization's culture, so you can dynamically realign your Strategic Human Assets to respond quickly in a turbulent world. This is the missed ingredient in most companies today, where they are in a hurry to change tactics and strategies, but forget to adjust their human assets. That is why initiatives fail most of the time. But Realignment of Strategic Human Assets should be as important to a strategist as execution.

## Create Unstoppable Momentum for Your Business

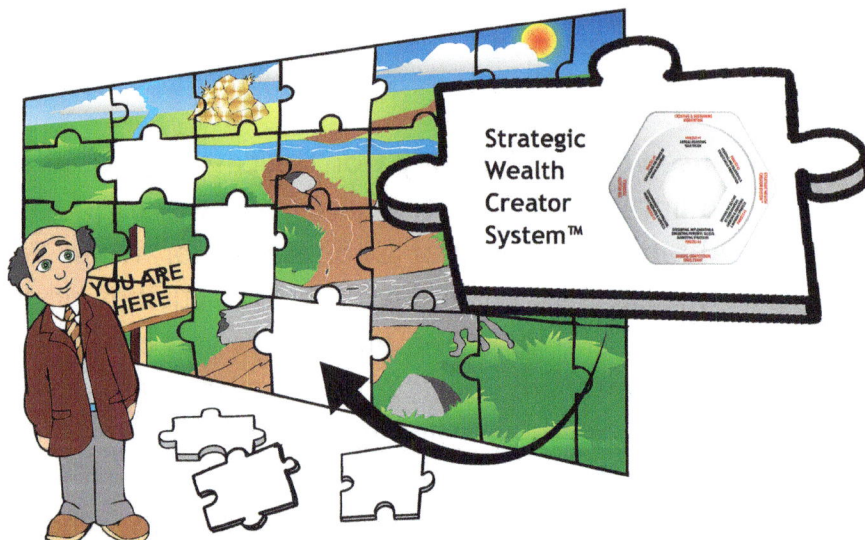

Simply put, each of the six processes is powerful in its own right. When you implement them together, you will find they create an unstoppable momentum for your business that essentially makes competition irrelevant. Suddenly, the market is chasing you – and it will never be able to catch up. But that will only happen if you make a firm commitment to follow each one of the six strategic thinking processes, and the proven concepts supporting them, so they become embedded in the culture of your organization.

Think of it this way: the six processes are a framework, a skeleton for you to flesh out with your organization's own culture, knowledge, and skills. Each organization following these processes will flesh them out in a unique way – but all of the elements to thrive in a fast-moving world are there, at your fingertips!

## Jay's Perspective

One reason I love working with Carlos is his practical, real-world, strategic-thinking orientation.

His system is so powerful because as a former CEO of multinational companies, he has lived it himself – creating success after success in turbulent times. Then, as an advisor and mentor to global CEOs and executive teams, he has proven it over and over again, in company after company, industry after industry, all over the world.

*Jay Abraham*

Here is how Carlos thinks – it will give you an idea of the profound insight, inspiration, and attention to detail that he has brought to bear on creating the Strategic Wealth Creator System™.

To create a process for solving a business problem, Carlos follows a rigorous, four-step, proven path.

- First, he establishes the facts, using the same powerful Socratic questions he teaches in our program to establish what is true and what is merely assumption or wishful thinking.
- Second, he develops and verifies his hypothesis into a holistic idea, by applying it in the context of an organization-wide ecosystem rather than a collection of parts.

- Third, he expands his idea into a concept – and validates it in the market.

- Fourth, based on his more than forty years of leading and managing organizations around the world, he converts his concept into a strategic thinking process – a step-by-step template that you and your organization can use to execute the concept.

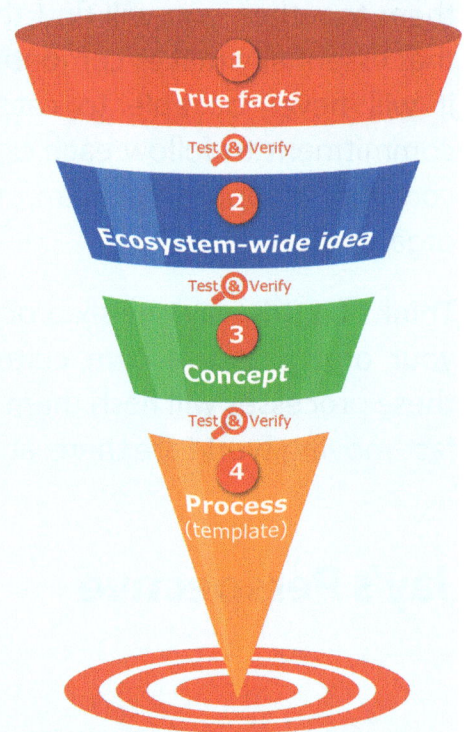

Carlos followed the same four steps to convert many of my concepts, such as Three Ways to Grow a Business and the Strategy of Preeminence, into powerful processes that will transform your business ecosystem.

The ecosystem perspective built into this system is quite unique and powerful, by the way. It steps you through how to build an entire web of products or services – like you see when you buy from Apple or Google or Amazon – where all the products are masterfully coordinated so that you buy the first one, then keep on buying time after time, preempting your competition.

If you have attended educational programs or seminars, you know that the process orientation of Step 4 is also quite unique.

Carlos tells us:

**"A concept without a process is like a boat without a rudder. You won't get where you want to go without it!"**

But most management books and programs today just drop the concept and run. They give you theory, but no way to apply it.

This is where Carlos' first-hand, successful experience as a CEO is so important. He understands what you need to lead your business – both the background knowledge and the practical, hands-on, step-by-step guidance on how to apply each process, how to make it work, and how to get it adopted so it is implemented consistently throughout your organization. This is the real world speaking, not a professor or guru, not a theory that might work in some ideal world – but practical processes that were created so that you can adapt them to your real world circumstances – and you can keep adapting them again and again, so you stay on course even as external circumstances change.

I think Carlos has nailed it, and I think that's because Carlos really understands the practical realities of a CEO's world. He understands that you need to learn – but you also need to do. You need to change your own paradigms and mental models – but you also need to bring the rest of the organization along with you, so they get it too. You need to accomplish all of this with care and thought, not in some costly but less-than-memorable one-week seminar or academic brain-dump. But at the same time, you can't take a few weeks or semesters off of work – and neither can your management team – just to study obsolete theories that applied to a bygone world.

Before Carlos was a CEO, he studied engineering. I think it shows. Carlos didn't just create a system, he also packaged it into a "learning and doing" program that shows you each strategic-thinking process, gives you the powerful, proven tools you'll need to keep you moving forward, and then takes you through, step-by-step, as you implement the program with your own executive team. Carlos calls this program "Creative Leadership for Turbulent Times." I think it's that last missing piece of the roadmap you've been looking for.

See for yourself.

*"I had the opportunity to learn from gurus such as Gary Hamel, Michael Porter.... However, they don't offer any advice on how to actually use those concepts in organizations. It was very different with you.*

*"You were able to explain to us all your concepts, and how to apply each one of them in our company. We appreciate your generosity very much."*

**ALFREDO ESPONDA ESPINOSA**
**CEO & MANAGING DIRECTOR, CENCADE, MEXICO**

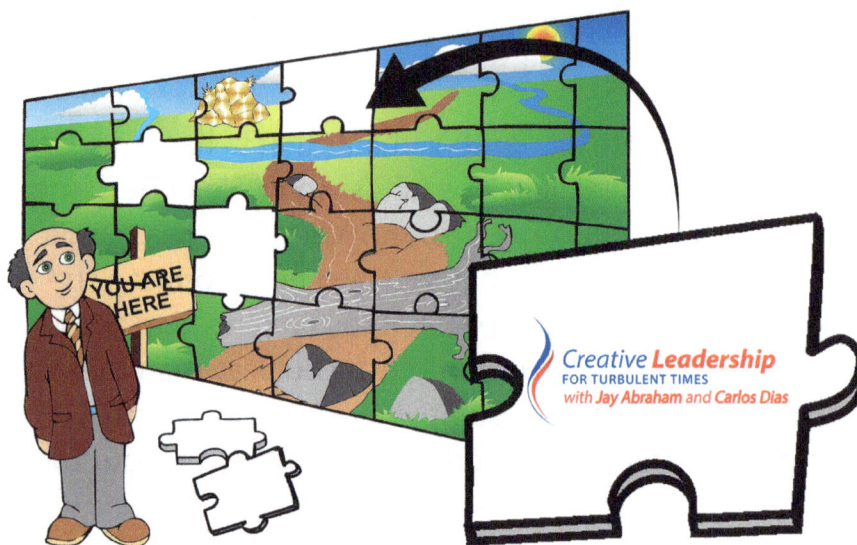

# Each Process Is a Separate Learning Module

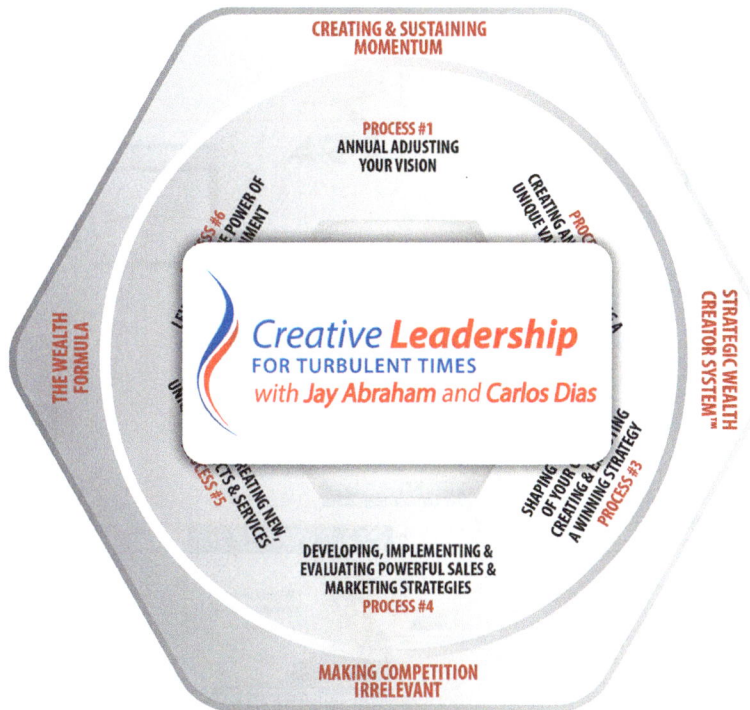

In Creative Leadership for Turbulent Times, each strategic thinking process in the Strategic Wealth Creator System™ is broken out as a separate learning-and-doing module, and because Carlos and Jay understand that both **you and your team** need to participate in the learning and doing, they have packaged into the program **everything** you need to learn, align your team, and implement each process.

That's *everything*, including the ability to share the benefits with up to twenty-one of your key executives, at no additional cost.

# Elements of the Program

Each module contains more than three hours of **state-of-the-art, interactive eLearning**, available anytime and anywhere you are ready to learn, on an iPad, laptop, or desktop computer. The eLearning features video tips from Carlos Dias and Jay Abraham and stunning photos and diagrams, accompanied by professional audio narration. It is designed for learning in the real world – so you can resume where you left off the last time, without skipping a beat. You can view an entire module of the program in sequence – that's the recommended method – or you can use the menus to navigate to a block and topic of your choice.

A full-color **Strategic Thinking Guidebook™**, accessible online, reviews many of the key points in the eLearning and lays out how to implement what you learned, step by step. It has been designed not to be a stand-alone learning tool, but a powerful companion to the interactive eLearning system.

At each implementation step, you'll enter your findings into a set of electronic **Mastermind Maps™** – set up to make it easy to capture your insights and share them with other executives or with your Board. The Mastermind Maps™ are designed to let your team work together, no matter whether you are co-located or in remote offices. They will present you with a series of critical Socratic questions which required over ten years of experience to compile – and they will get your team thinking, adjusting, and answering in a new way. Don't worry; this will not be just a sterile exercise. It is in these completed maps where you will find the solutions to your business problems.

To help you think through and evaluate your ideas, you will also receive dozens of proprietary **Strategic Calculators™,** along with instructions on when and how to use them. You and your team will be able to use these Strategic Calculators™ again and again during your decision-making meetings as well as in your daily work. Just enter your own data and see where your business stands. Or change your assumptions and instantly see and share the results with your staff. Can you visualize the impact on your culture as you and your executive teams learn and try different scenarios together as you create your own unique and powerful strategy?

Also included in each module are up to three hours of special skill-building **Virtual Mentoring Sessions™**, always available online for your convenience, to help you translate your new skills to your business environment – or share a new skill set with others in your organization.

Of course, included with the program is Carlos and Jay's, *The CEO Who Sees around Corners* – their new book that explains the thought-leadership required to be a great executive in the twenty-first century. This book, which comes with your program package, is a must-read for every executive before starting the program.

# Recommended Flow

To get the most out of each module, here is the flow that Carlos and Jay recommend:

**Set a goal to complete each module in approximately three to four months**. That is a realistic goal, even in the busiest work environment. You cannot become an accurate creative thinker leader for the twenty-first century in only one week! Creative Leadership for Turbulent Times has not been designed for CEOs hoping to immediately absorb so many powerful concepts and processes. Here is why:

**Month 1 is time for Discovery**. We recommend that the CEO and up to 20 key senior executives learn on their own. Each of you, independently, views the eLearning, checks out the Strategic Calculators™, Mastermind Maps™, and Virtual Mentoring Sessions™, and reviews the step-by-step instructions in the Strategic Thinking Guidebook™. During this time, you will find yourself generating new ideas for how to apply these concepts in your business. The Discovery period is exciting – but it is also a time for discipline. So don't rush forward too quickly to apply your new ideas. Don't settle for merely being aware or informed. Take this month to study and apply your mind purposefully to acquiring knowledge and wisdom. The program has already been compressed into a fast-track to leadership for you, so don't try to compress it further.

**Month 2 is time for Conceptualizing**, forming an idea of the interplay of concepts and processes in your own mind. In this month, you and your senior executives will still be working on your own – but now you are beginning to play with some of the critical thinking exercises in the Strategic Thinking Guidebook™. This is the time when you begin to build some starter ideas – ideas that you can capture so you can share them later with others. This is also the time to set up your Mastermind Group Alliance – one of the Virtual Mentoring Sessions™ breaks down for you exactly how to select the right people, what the CEO's role should be as sponsor of the group, and how to prepare participants to facilitate their own group sessions – just about anything you might need to know in order to run a successful Mastermind Group Alliance. Additionally, in Month 2, you also will have the opportunity to interact with Carlos and Jay directly, emailing questions, participating in live webinars or viewing dynamic, frequently updated content on the Executive Learning Systems Web site.

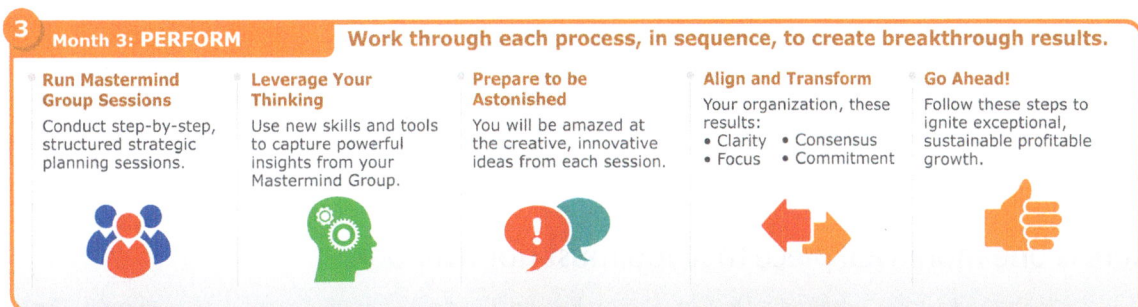

**3** **Month 3: PERFORM** — Work through each process, in sequence, to create breakthrough results.

| **Run Mastermind Group Sessions** | **Leverage Your Thinking** | **Prepare to be Astonished** | **Align and Transform** | **Go Ahead!** |
|---|---|---|---|---|
| Conduct step-by-step, structured strategic planning sessions. | Use new skills and tools to capture powerful insights from your Mastermind Group. | You will be amazed at the creative, innovative ideas from each session. | Your organization, these results:<br>• Clarity • Consensus<br>• Focus • Commitment | Follow these steps to ignite exceptional, sustainable profitable growth. |

**Months 3 and 4 are time to Perform**. Now it is time to apply your new strategic thinking processes within your organization. Working together, as a Mastermind Group of senior executives and others with special expertise, you will work step-by-step through the exercises in your Strategic Thinking Guidebook™. At this point, you will already be familiar with the exercises and may even have some preliminary answers in the back of your mind. But you will find that, working together, you will quickly leapfrog to new, innovative insights. It's a painstaking, exhausting process – one that is guaranteed to get you and your team excited and inspired!

## The Program in Context

The processes you will learn in Creative Leadership for Turbulent Times are a crucial missing piece of your road map to find the motherlode of hidden wealth in your business.

But there is one more vital piece that you must not overlook.

## Using Mastermind Group Alliance

For best results, Carlos and Jay absolutely encourage you to implement the program within a Mastermind Group Alliance. Carlos has personally implemented these processes with thousands of CEOs and senior executives – so he can tell you from first-hand experience: a Mastermind Group Alliance is the best way to maximize the intellectual capital that you will gain in this program, by leveraging what you learn in the program across all the knowledge, understanding, and wisdom available in your organization.

Think about it:

A Mastermind Group Alliance is the best insurance against getting trapped by preconceptions, false assumptions, or denial.

Your Mastermind Group Alliance will force you to answer powerful, carefully chosen Socratic questions that force you outside of your comfort zone.

Albert Einstein once said:

*"If I had an hour to solve a problem and my life depended on the solution, I would spend the first fifty-five minutes determining the proper question to ask, for once I know the proper question, I could solve the problem in less than five minutes."*

**ALBERT EINSTEIN**

Jay and Carlos spent years proving and adjusting each one of the Socratic questions in each module. You will be able to answer each one of these questions and consider ideas that you would never have thought of on your own. They will help you to see issues from different perspectives – to force you out of that echo-chamber inside your head.

You, as CEO, won't have to adopt their ideas – but you will have the benefit of listening and thinking about them. You'll be richer for the experience – you'll find it more enjoyable and rewarding to do this work with a group. You'll also find that you feel more confident about your decisions, because you will have had the benefit of the best minds in your organization, all focused on solving the same problems.

There is one more benefit that you absolutely must not underestimate. It's another missing piece that stands between you and the hidden wealth in your organization.

# Become a Culture Warrior!

*"When 'meaning' of a workplace is lacking, employee energy dissipates in the form of office politics, ego-management, and passive-aggressive avoidance of tough issues. CEOs and senior executives with meaning in what they do are five times more productive at their peak than they are on average."*

**SUSIE CRANSTON AND SCOTT KELLER**
*"INCREASING THE 'MEANING QUOTIENT' OF WORK" MCKINSEY,* **FEBRUARY 2013**

That's what the Mastermind Group Alliance will do for your culture: inspiring exceptional levels of energy, self-confidence, and both individual and group productivity. The Mastermind Group Alliance should be one of the most important tools in any twenty-first century leader's arsenal, because it allows you to instill a sense of "meaning" throughout your organization. Jay and Carlos have seen what happens when meaning is missing – we've all seen it: the lack of commitment, the confused response, the underwhelming and half-hearted performance that results when people in the organization don't understand why they are doing the tasks they have been asked to do.

*"Education and intelligence accomplish nothing without 'meaning.' It is just as important to know 'why' as it is to know 'what.' Without commitment, you can accomplish nothing in life.*

*"Have a meaning in everything you do, and confidence in your own abilities; work smart, be committed... and there is nothing you cannot accomplish."*

**CARLOS DIAS**

Within a Mastermind Group Alliance framework, you can know that the "meaning" message gets through. You can know because each executive in the Alliance will be fully participating, will see the direct relevance of each strategic thinking session to the success of the organization, and will understand both what plan you are adopting and why you have chosen it.

The nature of the Mastermind Group is to create a collaborative atmosphere – where ideas are generated by the group, agreed to by the group – in other words, there is group buy-in.

Then, after the ideas are approved and adopted by your Board, that same group of key executives is ready to swing into action – already aligned, and already committed to making the new ideas work.

They become your culture warriors. They are the engine that will defeat resistance to change, clarify misinterpretations, and keep your new initiatives on the right track.

## An Aligned Organization

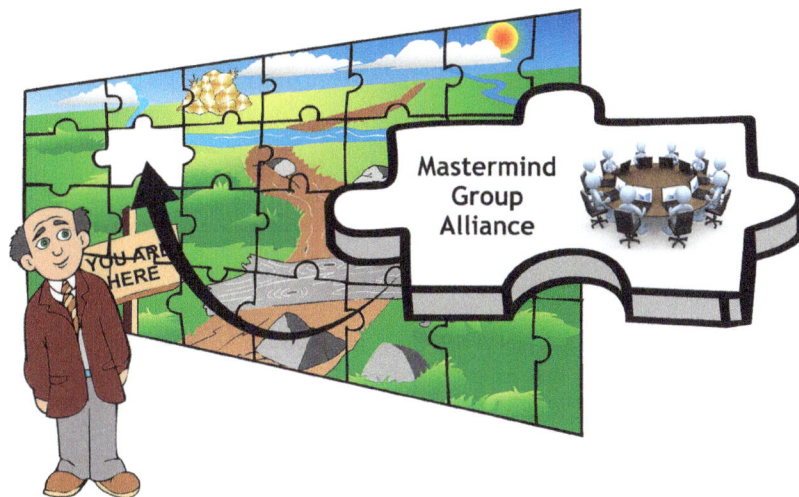

Working within a Mastermind Group is like culture insurance – so you know with certainty that your strategies will be implemented with enthusiasm and vigor, at every level of the organization.

You will finally have the vision, leadership skill, processes, and people in place to find the motherlode of hidden wealth – the pathway to a highly profitable, sustainable business for you and your family to enjoy, even in turbulent times.

# The Choice is Yours

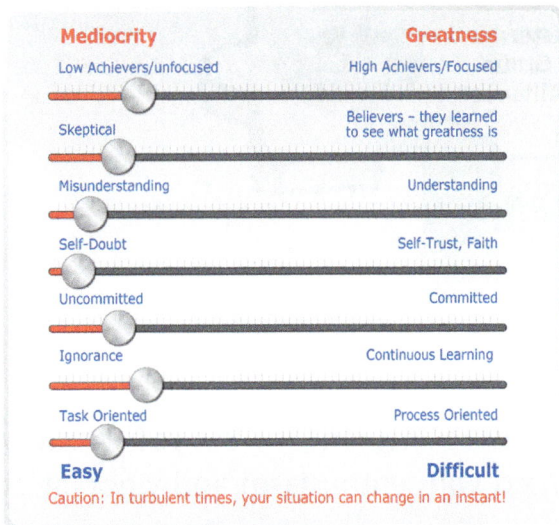

Our friend John wanted to transform his company – but he was frozen by insecurity. He had a vision of becoming a great leader – but he didn't have a roadmap.

*Carlos Dias*

Until now. Now John can see where he wants to go – and how to get there. With Creative Leadership for Turbulent Times, John has a systematic way to develop himself and to develop his organization.

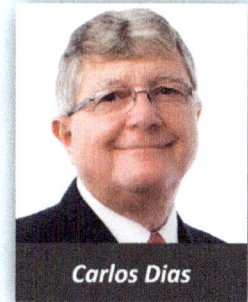

By following the six strategic-thinking processes of the Strategic Wealth Creator System™, in conjunction with a Mastermind Group Alliance, John finally knows that he has put his business on the right path – he has found the hidden wealth in his organization – and secured the future for his family and shareholders. After months and years of self-doubt and frustration, John has learned how to lead his organization in turbulent times. He has finally achieved peace of mind.

How about you?

Are you ready to settle for mediocrity? That looks like the easier route, but it is a route to nowhere.

Greatness is harder. It takes time, commitment, and courage.

But the reward is beyond price. Finally you'll know that you have achieved your potential – the potential you were born to achieve. You'll have the confidence that comes from building a new blueprint for success for your business. You'll have experienced the thrill of transforming your organization from market-follower to market-leader, with a new culture that is agile and ready to adapt to future challenges. You'll have earned the satisfaction of transforming your business into a highly profitable, growing concern – one that can sustain your family well into the future.

Don't settle. Take the first step to greatness. Jay and I are here to show you the way.

It will be a challenging route; you will find yourself travelling outside of your comfort zone. But you will always know that you are on the right path – because Carlos and I have travelled this path with so many multinational CEOs and executives before you – so we can guarantee that we can get you where you want to go safely.

How can we make such a unique promise? We'll explain in the next section.

# PART 4

## Uniqueness

 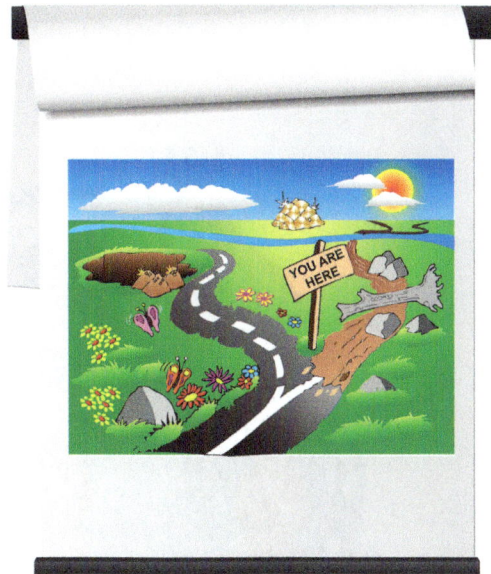

**Remember John?** When we first met him, John had been struggling to find a way – a sure and certain way – to stop settling for mediocrity and put his business onto a path that would lead to sustainable, profitable wealth and growth. But at the time, John did not know what to do next.

*Jay Abraham*

John knew that standing still and staying mediocre wasn't really an option – he was just handing opportunity after opportunity to his competitors, losing more ground every day. So he was willing and eager to do what it took to change. But like most CEOs, John couldn't afford to try and fail. His business simply could not afford rookie mistakes. He needed to know with certainty that he was on the right path before he set out.

In Part 4, Carlos and I will show John – and you – how to get on the right path to succeed in turbulent times.

## A Scarcity

*"There is a scarcity of senior executives who have the experience needed to deal with today's unique and highly complex problems!"*

**JACK FRITZ**
*TALENT MANAGEMENT MAGAZINE, DECEMBER 2012*

It seems that all over the world there are more CEOs like John than ever before – leaders who feel out of their depth in today's turbulent business environment.

They are right to feel that way. Few senior executives are equipped to cope with today's pace of change.

# The New Imperative

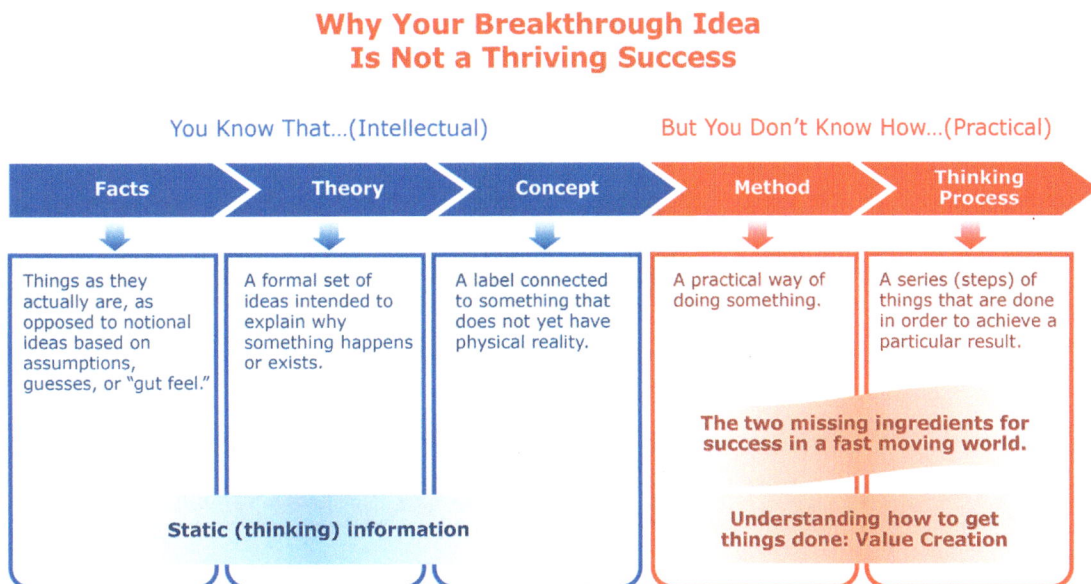

**Why Your Breakthrough Idea Is Not a Thriving Success**

You Know That…(Intellectual)      But You Don't Know How…(Practical)

| Facts | Theory | Concept | Method | Thinking Process |
|---|---|---|---|---|
| Things as they actually are, as opposed to notional ideas based on assumptions, guesses, or "gut feel." | A formal set of ideas intended to explain why something happens or exists. | A label connected to something that does not yet have physical reality. | A practical way of doing something. | A series (steps) of things that are done in order to achieve a particular result. |

Static (thinking) information

**The two missing ingredients for success in a fast moving world.**

**Understanding how to get things done: Value Creation**

**Continuous learning is no longer an option.
It's an imperative for every senior executive.**

If you consider what senior executives need to know in order to do their jobs, it's not surprising that there is a disconnect. They need to know both how to create exciting, profitable new ideas for their business, and they need to know how to implement them. In other words, they need both intellectual knowledge and practical knowledge.

That would be a lot, even if everything were standing still. But in today's fast-moving world, knowledge is exploding.

Continuous learning is no longer an option. It's an imperative for every senior executive, in every organization that wants to grow and thrive.

## What Are John's Options?

So what are John's options? What is the most effective – and most practical – way for him and his executive team to get the updated knowledge and skills they so desperately need?

## Business School?

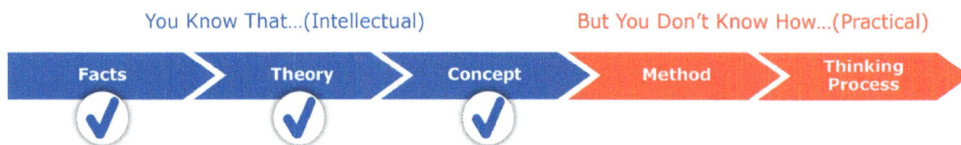

You Know That...(Intellectual)        But You Don't Know How...(Practical)

| Facts | Theory | Concept | Method | Thinking Process |
| ✓ | ✓ | ✓ | | |

*"Aside from the sheer cost of earning a two-year MBA... management school graduates are finding that their skills and training are not ideally matched to the needs of global corporations that have undergone rapid changes."*

**RAKESH KHURANA**
**PROFESSOR, HARVARD SCHOOL OF BUSINESS**
*STRATEGY AND BUSINESS,* **JAN. 21, 2013**

The first thing that springs to John's mind is sending some of his key executives back to school.

Many senior executives learn their craft at business school – from theoreticians rather than experienced business people. Their professors derived their theories from thorough and careful study… but only of what has succeeded or failed *in the past*. While they say they teach how to apply the concepts, the case studies the professors teach from are carefully constructed to reinforce their theories. They indeed demonstrate how the theories have been applied successfully – but only assuming that conditions are as they had been *in the past*.

Real-world experience – and learning to apply strategic foresight – are nowhere on the curriculum.

Sending executives for an MBA requires a huge outlay of cash, not to mention a significant investment in time. The return on investment for this option is poor. Is it any wonder that today's MBA graduates, after spending upwards of $100,000 plus lodging and living expenses, leave school unprepared to face the revolution and upheaval that are staples of life today?

## One-Dimensional Seminars?

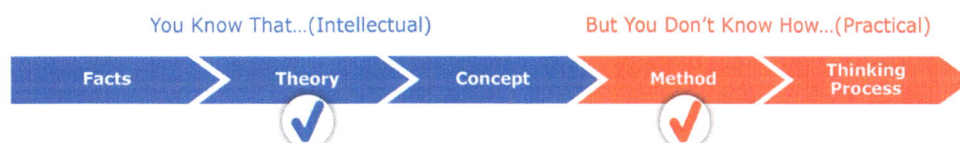

You Know That…(Intellectual)        But You Don't Know How…(Practical)

| Facts | Theory | Concept | Method | Thinking Process |

*"Buying a 'generic' leadership program without regard for market challenges is akin to buying performance management software and ignoring cultural biases that block employees from adopting its use."*

**JACK FRITZ**
*TALENT MANAGEMENT MAGAZINE*, DECEMBER 2011

Many senior executives look for a quick fix to their lack of preparation by enrolling in post-graduate workshops or seminars from well-known management gurus or professors. But these programs tend to be one-dimensional, showcasing the guru's particular area of expertise – with no thought about how to integrate that expertise in the real-world pressure cooker that today's CEOs face. At the end of the program, an executive has yet another souvenir binder – but no practical ideas on how to run their business.

## Individual Self-Development?

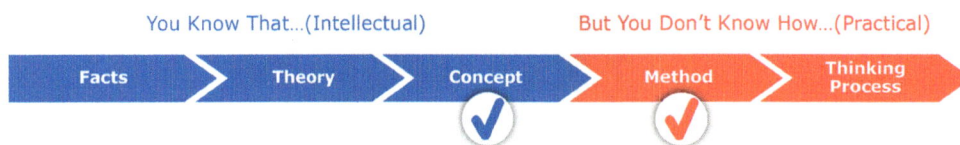

You Know That...(Intellectual)   But You Don't Know How...(Practical)

Facts ▸ Theory ▸ Concept ▸ Method ▸ Thinking Process

*"The only conditions in which experience is the best teacher are the ones in which no change takes place."*

**RUSSEL ACKOFF**

Of course, many senior executives and even board members will tell you that their approach to self-development is to learn from experience. It's a dangerous delusion – like learning to drive a car by looking only in the rear-view mirror. You can get pretty good at it if you practice – but it will only work as long as the road ahead is just like the road behind you. In turbulent times, the landscape keeps shifting. If you only know how to look backward, you inevitably are going to crash!

## The Disconnect: Individual Development

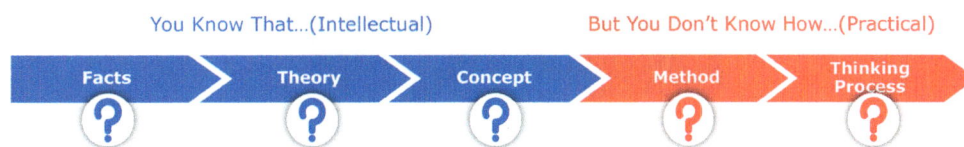

Then there are the CEOs and Board Members who say, "I don't need to worry about updating my skills and knowledge. I expect my staff to keep abreast of changes."

They look at knowledge and learning as the responsibility of their individual employees – instead of as a valuable organizational asset.

But in turbulent times, the shelf-life of organizational knowledge is shorter. Successful businesses have learned to exploit this fact, installing systems to continuously develop and nurture organizational learning, so they can continue to outrun their competition. But organizational learning only works if it is truly part of the culture – and that means it has to start from the top, with CEOs, senior executives, and board members who themselves are committed to learning new leadership skills and concepts.

*"The Gottlieb Duttweiler Foundation found that only 20% of knowledge available to an organization is actually used…. "Competitive advantage stems from the firm-specific configuration of its intangible knowledge."*

**CHARLES EGBU AND KATE BOTTERILL**

## What Is Needed?

| | |
|---|---|
| • ~~Backward-looking~~ | • Forward-looking |
| • ~~One-Dimensional approaches~~ | • Adaptive approaches |
| • ~~Theories~~ | • Proven, Practical Processes |
| • ~~Individual Knowledge~~ | • Intellectual Asset |

**AGILITY**

Today's leaders need a program that teaches – not yesterday's approaches; not one-dimensional solutions that only work in unique circumstances or in specific industries; not grand theories that are unworkable in the real world; and not individual knowledge that can't be shared.

To succeed in a turbulent world, today's leaders need to learn the art of **agility**.

- They need to learn how to navigate by looking forward, rather than backward, so they can position their organizations to take advantage of new opportunities.
- They need to find approaches that can be adapted quickly, so they are able to respond in the face of an ever-increasing pace of change.
- They need practical, proven processes – processes they can use to lead and guide their organizations to continuously out-compete, out-innovate, and out-perform their markets.

- They need a way to change their culture in order to nurture, develop, and share knowledge – because the organization that learns how to exploit that remaining 80% of its intellectual assets will have an unstoppable advantage over the competition.

## Where Can You Learn Leadership Ability?

### JAY ABRAHAM

**"Some of the biggest entrepreneurial success stories of the last 20 years have been masterminded by Jay Abraham..."**

- ANTHONY ROBBINS -

**"Jay is... a brilliant marketing genius that knows more ways to make money for business than anyone I know."**

- T. HARV EKAR -

**"If there were a Hall of Fame for business and marketing, Jay would be there. He is the ultimate business coach."**

- FRAN TARKENTON -

### CARLOS DIAS

**"(wrote the) handbook for business and profitability in turbulent times."**

- BRIAN TRACY -

**"His system is... a 'must know' in today's rapidly changing, highly competitive world."**

- EMANUELE PORTOLESE -
*Founder, Brett Sports International*

**"This new way of reflecting helped (senior executives with more than 30 years experience) to fully utilize their own experience and knowledge for the future of their company."**

- JOSE JAN GARCIA -
*President, Gentil S.A.*

**More testimonials at: http://www.executivelearningsystems.com/testimonials/**

But where do you learn leadership agility?

Where do you learn how to make the profound paradigm shift required of leaders in order to succeed in turbulent times?

Back in 2009, Carlos Dias and Jay Abraham surveyed the situation and realized that no such program existed. Jay, recognized by *Forbes* magazine as a world marketing and strategic genius, had witnessed business after business reeling under the impact of turbulent change – and saw the pain their leaders felt as they worked themselves back from the brink. Carlos, himself a successful multinational CEO and mentor to senior executives around the world, was a process-master – a wizard at breaking theories and strategies into practical, step-by-step, implementable approaches – approaches that turned "stuck" companies into profitable engines of growth. Together, Jay and Carlos realized that they had the rare combination – the breadth and depth, the theory and practical experience, the passion and commitment – that was required to create a program like no other.

## State-of-the-Art Program

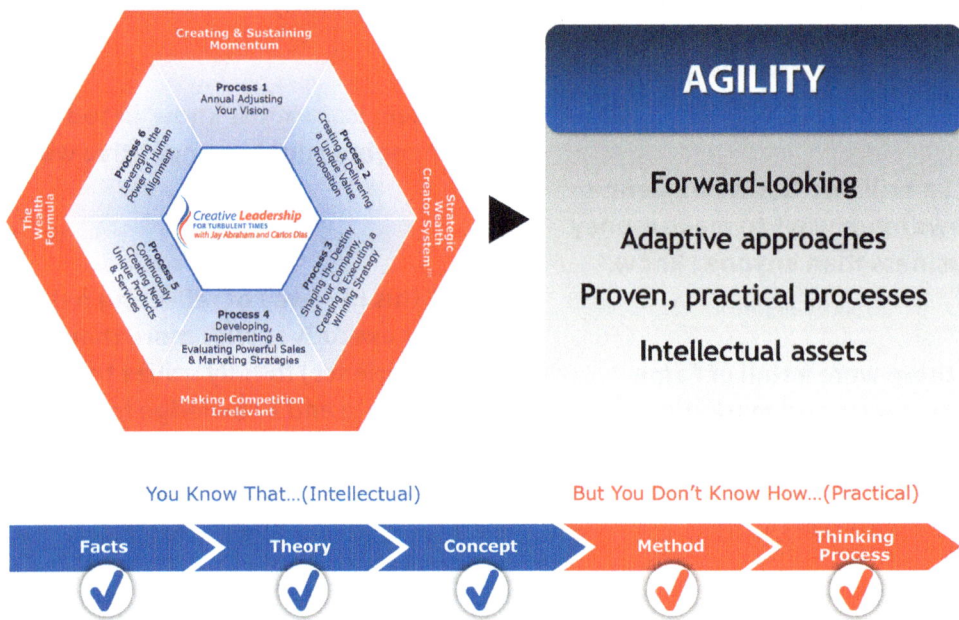

That's why Carlos and Jay created a state-of-the-art eLearning program from the ground up. They built it in response to what the market told them – the real needs of real CEOs and executives around the world, all struggling to lead in an uncertain world.

They constructed it for agility and to make an organization profitably thrive in turbulent times.

It was a huge undertaking, working with a team of experts over a five-year period, to release the program after testing it with their clients.

# Critical Thinking Toolkit

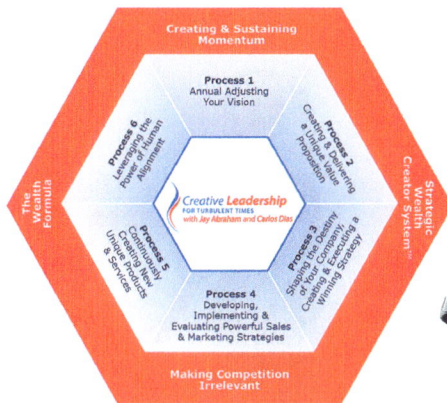

Here's why. In a turbulent world, you cannot survive if you have mastered only one tool. It doesn't matter whether your hammer is stronger, more precise, or made of solid gold. If you need a different tool, that hammer is not going to help you.

In a turbulent world, where you cannot predict which tool you will need tomorrow, what you need is a **mental toolkit** – a critical thinking process, based on a flexible set of proven concepts and methods, so no matter what comes at you, you will be prepared with the concepts, skills, and know-how to select the right tool at the right time and use it in the right way – to keep your business growing and thriving as you move forward.

# Agile Tools for a Leader

Grow Your Leadership Mindset
Take a Quantum Leap to Manifest Your Leadership Potential

Creative Leadership for Turbulent Times was created specifically for CEOs like John. You remember: John's business was stuck in neutral. John was stuck too – stuck in his comfort zone, lacking the confidence in his ability to make the right strategic decisions for the business, and paralyzed by the fear of not knowing how to respond if an unexpected event should come along.

But with Creative Leadership for Turbulent Times, John's mindset changed. His comfort zone expanded. Even though times were uncertain, after reaching stage five John had new certainty in his ability to lead, he had the knowledge at his fingertips to position his business for a more successful, more profitable future, and he had the proven tools at his command, so he was ready to respond quickly and keep his business on the right track.

In other words, John no longer felt like he had to be a victim of circumstances. Instead, he could once again be the master of his fate – and the fate of his organization. Using the concepts and tools in Creative Leadership for Turbulent Times, he could essentially write the future of his organization.

# Be Prepared to Thrive, No Matter What Your Fortune!

That kind of peace of mind doesn't come easily. It must be earned.

But when John had put in the effort, by the time he had learned the concepts and worked through the strategic thinking processes with his Mastermind Group Alliance, he experienced for himself what CEO greatness really means.

Whatever fortune threw at him or his business, John knew that he was prepared to deal with it – that he could identify and seize the opportunity in any situation to ensure a successful future for his business.

On the following pages, you'll see some of today's common business "fortunes" John (and you) might encounter, and preview a few of the proven tools, processes, and concepts that will be at your fingertips as you react to a quickly changing business environment.

You'll learn these and many other exciting business ideas – all presented in context, so you understand how to integrate them into your overall business strategy, and all broken down into step-by-step activities, so you know not only when and why to use the technique, but also how to customize it to your environment and how to teach it to your management team.

What about you? In an uncertain world, are you ready and able to lead your organization to survive and thrive – no matter what the future throws into your path?

Read on to learn more.

*Your current products will soon stop supporting growth.*

*You are using yesterday's thinking. Update your paradigm or lose your business.*

*You cannot thrive if you insist on doing everything on your own.*

*You are falling behind the pack in technical knowledge.*

*If you do too much, you will not be able to do anything.*

*Your competitors are picking off your best customers, one by one.*

*Your product is old, tired, and stale.*

*The surest path to the top of the mountain is to find a guide who can show you the way.*

*When evaluating ROI, consider the Return as well as the Investment.*

*Trust but verify. – Ronald Reagan*

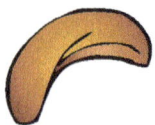

## Fortune Cookie #1

*Your current products will soon stop supporting growth.*

Do you know how to refocus your company for "endless" profitable growth?

The formula exists. Carlos and Jay call it "The Wealth Algorithm." It's a formula most CEOs learned in business school – but no one showed them how to apply it to fuel endless, continuous growth.

➲ You can learn more about the Wealth Algorithm in Module 1 of Creative Leadership for Turbulent Times.

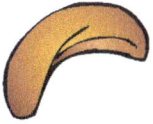

## Fortune Cookie #2

*You are using yesterday's thinking.*
*Update your paradigm or lose your business.*

Do you know how to leverage your personal knowledge and skills, in order to maximize the profitable growth of your business?

Many CEOs are searching in vain for a magic wand that will turbocharge their thinking power. But the answer exists! Jay and Carlos explain how you can change your paradigm – by leveraging four key intellectual assets required for CEO greatness and applying the six strategic divergent thinking processes in the Strategic Wealth Creator System™.

⮲  Read about the four key intellectual assets in Carlos and Jay's new book, The CEO Who Sees around Corners. Learn about each of the six strategic divergent thinking processes in Modules 1-6 of Creative Leadership for Turbulent Times.

## Fortune Cookie #3

*You cannot thrive if you insist on doing everything on your own.*

Are you making the most out of your Relational Assets? Do you know how (and why) to fuel highly-profitable growth through trusted alliances?

The "not invented here" syndrome is yesterday's thinking. To survive today, you need to look beyond "traditional" boundaries to your entire value chain. Here's a hint: the answer is in your external ecosystem – but only if you know how to leverage those relationships.

⮲  Jay and Carlos' breakthrough approach to leveraging Relational Assets is unique and eye-opening. It's a foundational concept you'll learn about throughout Modules 1-6 of Creative Leadership for Turbulent Times.

# Fortune Cookie #4

*You are falling behind the pack in technical knowledge.*

Do you have a way to stay up-to-date in all of the key areas in your industry? Are you making the most out of the intellectual assets in your organization?

No individual in your organization can have "perfect knowledge." In fact, in turbulent times, that goal is more elusive than ever. To compensate, Jay and Carlos show you how to apply the Mastermind Group Alliance concept in order to gain maximum leverage from your organization's intellectual assets.

➲ You'll find step-by-step, templated processes for developing your organization's strengths by applying the Mastermind Group Alliance framework in exciting new ways. Learn how in Creative Leadership for Turbulent Times.

# Fortune Cookie #5

*If you do too much, you will not be able to do anything.*

Are you shaping your organization to be efficient when it should be effective? "Efficient" is doing things right. "Effective" is doing the right things. As a leader, your goal should be to identify and concentrate your organization's efforts on the areas in which you can be most effective and profitable.

Carlos and Jay have found that few CEOs know where they are making money today – much less where they should best concentrate tomorrow. Instead, they waste their organizations' time and treasure, chasing too many different types of customers for too little reward. To succeed, you need to develop a backbone – a "business backbone," that is – so you know both where to play, and even more importantly, where not to play.

➲ Module 1 of Creative Leadership for Turbulent Times is packed with tips on how to see where you are currently making money, what your current "Business Backbone" is, and how to work your current strategy in a way that makes you instantly become 16X more productive. In later modules, you'll explore how to select and fine-tune your "Business Backbone" and product strategy for exponential, sustainable profitable growth.

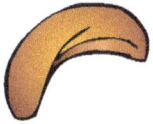

## Fortune Cookie #6

*Your competitors are picking off your best customers, one by one.*

How loyal are your customers? Are you one of those CEOs who feels sick inside every time you see a new competitor's ad campaign?

It is time to stop worrying about the competition and start preempting them! Jay and Carlos will show you straightforward, step-by-step strategic thinking processes that apply Jay Abraham's "Strategy of Preeminence" – and drive your competition crazy.

➲ Module 2 of Creative Leadership for Turbulent Times explains the Strategy of Preeminence and introduces strategic thinking processes to create an army of zealot clients who will happily purchase everything you offer.

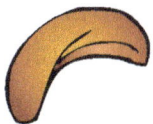

## Fortune Cookie #7

*Your product is old, tired, and stale.*

Are you innovating? Does your business have the creative juice needed to get customers excited in these highly-competitive times?

Jay and Carlos believe that every business can learn to be more creative – with the right leadership. They back up their opinion with step-by-step innovation-leadership processes and tools to help you light a fire under your product engineers and keep your competitors guessing. Unlike other innovation-leadership materials in the market, Jay and Carlos have crafted their process to make it ultra-usable – and integrate seamlessly with the rest of the processes in the Strategic Wealth Creator System™. Here's an easy-to-like feature: it's affordable – all processes in the system are included for one low price.

➲ Using the Strategic Value Innovation processes in Modules 2, 3, and 5 of Creative Leadership for Turbulent Times, you will learn how to create and release a continuous stream of innovative products that leave your competitors always playing catch-up.

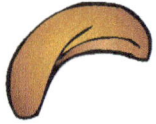

## Fortune Cookie #8

*The surest path to the top of the mountain is to find a guide who can show you the way.*

Every CEO wants to reach a level of greatness, but few can achieve greatness on their own. The rest, if they are lucky, find a guide with the experience and expertise to show them the way.

Who will you choose to guide you? If your answer is a business school or an MBA program, here is the bad news. Experts writing in the *Financial Times*, the *Wall Street Journal*, and even the *Harvard Business Review* all agree that academia is not the best place for CEOs and Senior Executives to learn the skills required in our turbulent world. Guru-seminars are too one-dimensional, too topic-specific, to be useful in developing a holistic strategic mindset.

Jay and Carlos have drawn upon their **extensive, real-world experience and expertise** to create a **practical, state of the art approach** to address the learning needs of C-Suite executives – in a way that actually reflects how business is conducted today. Convenient **eLearning** is available when and where you and your staff need it. An in-depth Virtual Mentoring Series™ is included for anyone who wants to go deeper. Proprietary **Strategic Calculators™** level the playing field – so you have the tools at your fingertips to test multiple strategies and financial outcomes. Carefully constructed **Strategic Thinking Guidebooks™** and online **Mastermind Maps™** give you all the tools you need to facilitate strategic-thinking sessions – whether your executive team is sitting across the room or on the other side of the world.

- ⮑ As turbulent times mean change keeps coming at you, you will also be given access to dynamic, up-to-the-minute live webinars and writings on timely topics that will keep you current.
- ⮑ In Jay and Carlos' Creative Leadership for Turbulent Times, you will find a complete system that has been created for both of your roles as a leader:
- ⮑ to learn, develop, and update your personal paradigm, and to lead your organization as you apply exciting, preeminent strategies for sustainable, profitable growth.

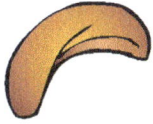

## Fortune Cookie #9

*When evaluating ROI, consider the*
*Return as well as the Investment.*

What would it cost you to go back to school for a few weeks, or send your team to a week-long seminar by a leading management guru? What would you have as a result of your investment, beside another certificate or binder?

Carlos and Jay have crafted their program to create the only real Return that matters: profitable business growth. Their value proposition is simple: here is everything a CEO needs to lead a strategic renaissance in your organization and secure a profitable future for yourself and your family.

We invite you to compare our price structure to other less complete options. We believe you will see the need is urgent and the value is incomparable.

Jay and Carlos believe that the greatest power in Creative Leadership for Turbulent Times happens when you leverage your intellectual assets by sharing the program with all of your key executives. That's why they have structured their pricing to make the "up to twenty-one executives" package the best value on the world market!

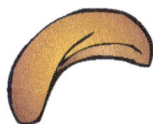

## Fortune Cookie #10

*Trust but verify. – Ronald Reagan*

We hope you are as excited as we are about creating a better, more profitable future for your business with Creative Leadership for Turbulent Times. But we also know that this program is not for everyone. It's practical – but it is also careful and thoughtful. It's convenient – but it still requires focused work. It's clear and step-by-step – but you have to apply the steps, hopefully within a Mastermind Group Alliance.

So even though you are eager to learn and apply and transform your organization's destiny… you may feel a certain sense of risk. You may be thinking to yourself, what if I start the program and it turns out not to be a good fit for us?

➲   We want you to be satisfied. You cannot know for sure until you have tried the program on for size. So we offer you a **simple, no-risk guarantee**.

# A Few Final Words

Remember where John started? He was facing a mountain of worry – with a business that was stuck and slowly being pulled down by the quicksand of turbulent change.

It took courage, commitment, perseverance, and a good, healthy dose of Jay and Carlos' strategic thinking processes. But John stayed the course. He saw it through…

*Jay Abraham*

…and good things happened.

His business? It's stronger than it has ever been before. He sells internationally now. He sells a narrower range of products these days, but his current line is more profitable. He particularly enjoys watching his competitors try desperately to compete against him by lowering their prices – they are so predictable. He just leapfrogs right over them with one new product after another. They can't out-guess him and they can't outrun him.

His team is happier these days, too. They understand what they are doing and why they are doing it. John can see they are exhilarated and enthusiastic about the future. John is excited to watch them develop. He is also relieved to know that, when he retires, he has a strong bench ready to take his place and keep the business strong. These are all the junior executives that he decided to register into the program.

John's family definitely is pleased with the upward trajectory of their dividends. It's nice to be the golden boy of the family again! John is happy to know that his family legacy is secured for years to come.

Is his life perfect now? Not quite. John's golf game is still lousy. But he sleeps better than ever. He enjoys his family more, and his appetite is great – particularly for fortune cookies.

That is what Creative Leadership for Turbulent Times did for John.

# Transform Your Destiny

We are so excited to offer you a subscription to Creative Leadership for Turbulent Times.

We believe, with all our hearts, that the program will be a transformative experience for you and your business.

**Try it** and you will transform your vision.

**Use it** and you'll transform your strategic approach.

**Embrace it** and you will transform your organization's destiny.

Carlos Dias

**Carlos Dias**

**Jay Abraham**

To take your first step on the path to success in a fast-moving world, visit:
*http://creativeleadershipforturbulenttimes.com/mlreader/*

CPSIA information can be obtained at www.ICGtesting.com
Printed in the USA
LVOW02*0830060214

372578LV00001B/2/P